AARON ZWAS

TRANSITION TO *INDEPENDENCE*

USE the T2I PLAN to LIVE and WORK on YOUR TERMS in the NEW IDEA ECONOMY

Published by Advantage, Charleston, South Carolina.
Member of Advantage Media Group.

ADVANTAGE is a registered trademark and the Advantage colophon is a trademark of Advantage Media Group, Inc.

Printed in the United States of America.

ISBN: 978-1-59932-522-4
LCCN: 2015956105

This publication is designed to provide accurate and authoritative information in regard to the subject matter covered. It is sold with the understanding that the publisher is not engaged in rendering legal, accounting, or other professional services. If legal advice or other expert assistance is required, the services of a competent professional person should be sought.

 Advantage Media Group is proud to be a part of the Tree Neutral® program. Tree Neutral offsets the number of trees consumed in the production and printing of this book by taking proactive steps such as planting trees in direct proportion to the number of trees used to print books. To learn more about Tree Neutral, please visit **www.treeneutral.com**. To learn more about Advantage's commitment to being a responsible steward of the environment, please visit **www.advantagefamily.com/green**

Advantage Media Group is a publisher of business, self-improvement, and professional development books and online learning. We help entrepreneurs, business leaders, and professionals share their Stories, Passion, and Knowledge to help others Learn & Grow. Do you have a manuscript or book idea that you would like us to consider for publishing? Please visit **advantagefamily.com** or call **1.866.775.1696.**

TRANSITION TO INDEPENDENCE

DEDICATION

To my father, from whom I learned the spirit of Independence
and how to make good on the promise of America.

To my wife and children,
I do this for each of you and for all of us together.

To my mentors, colleagues, and many clients.
I have learned so much from all of you. Thank you.

ABOUT THE AUTHOR

Aaron Zwas is a consulting journeyman with fifteen years of independent experience as a strategic technology advisor. His career, and the evolution of the T2I Plan, has spanned the lifestyles of a travel writer, young-and-single in New York City, and—currently—as a suburban married father of three.

Aaron manages his consulting practice, Zwas Group, from his home office and is able to spend significant time with his young family.

ACKNOWLEDGMENTS

Many people have contributed to the evolution of the T2I Plan and this book. I'd specifically like to thank...

My wife, Tootsie Olan, who (even as I write this) consistently put in extra hours with the family so that I had the time and space for this endeavor. You worked at least as hard as I did to make this a reality, Tootsie. Thank you. I can think of no one else with whom I'd rather "be independent."

My parents and siblings: Our strong family has always given me a reason to challenge the dynamics of traditional work so that I can spend more time with you. The T2I Plan is a direct response to my desire to be with you more often.

My late father-in-law, Michael Olan: I honor him and our families by building upon the foundations they have provided to us.

Lisa Dundon: It wasn't until I started writing this book that I realized what an enormous impact you had on my career by suggesting—and enabling—my first foray into Independence! Thank you, Lisa. It all started with you.

Dave, Maureen, and Jack: Thank you for the opportunities, the lessons, and the friendship.

Heather Turgeon: Your engaged feedback on the Introduction and first chapters of this book gave me the momentum I needed at a time when I thought this book might be just a passing phase. Thank you.

Tamara Altman: Your research heightened my understanding of the problem that T2I is intended to resolve, and your real-world experiences push the limits of what it means to be living in Independence. Thank you for the meticulous work and inspirational lifestyle.

Leslie Michelson and Christine Pride: Your feedback on emphasizing freedom was timely and well-heeded. Thank you.

Denis Boyles: Not only are you an expert practitioner of living in Independence, you gave this project the juice, insight, and voice it needed at just the right times. Thank you.

Scott Neville: You showed up when the ship was sinking fast, bailed out water, and steered a new course with a steady hand. Thank you for bringing us to shore, Scott.

The Advantage Team: Thank you for all of your efforts, large and small, that have brought this project to life. I am very happy to have found you, and I hope that we can embark on many projects together in the future.

—*Aaron Zwas*
December 2015

Table of Contents

Introduction

WHY YOU SHOULD READ THIS BOOK.

For one thing, it'll introduce you to a great way of life. For another, it'll show you how to live your working life as a free human being. And finally, it'll tell you how you can succeed doing what you most want to do. And get paid to do it.

Let me give you an example: I've been up since seven in the morning, playing with my kids, and helping to get them ready for a trip to the beach. We had a simple breakfast and watched some familiar cartoons in Spanish while my wife got in an hour of yoga. She then herded the kids off to a day of sand castles and splashing in the waves.

I grab my phone, open my laptop, and set up to work. It's cold back home, but it's eighty-three degrees and sunny here. I take a sip of strong coffee and listen to songs of unfamiliar birds around me. I'm barefoot and sitting at a quiet table at a resort in Cancun. After taking a quick moment to write this intro for you, I'll get to work. Today is Tuesday, and by about 12:30 p.m., I'll be done for the day and go join my family.

What do I do for work? I'm a consultant. And you know what? You can be one, too.

There are millions of us out there, living by our wits and flourishing. In the last four decades, independent consulting has been one of the biggest growth areas in professional employment. When we include independent consulting in the broader field of freelancing, the numbers are eye opening: An estimated 33 percent of the American

In the last four decades, independent consulting has been one of the biggest growth areas in professional employment.

workforce currently consider themselves freelancers, and that number is expected to grow to about 50 percent by 2020.

Independent consultants are becoming a mainstay of the modern workforce, injecting businesses and organizations with fresh ideas, bringing expertise to overworked and harried C-suite denizens, and creating a class of pioneering super-employees who are looking into the future not only for the benefit of those who retain them but for their own independence and livelihood as well. A smart consultant can see through the fog of office politics and look at a business from an informed, aerial view. He or she can monetize intelligence and experience in ways never seen before. A great consultant can gain freedom and independence through helping others navigate a sea of problems by turning a stormy economic climate into something as smooth and peaceful as the bright blue Caribbean spreading out ahead of me.

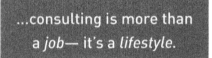

...consulting is more than a *job*— it's a *lifestyle.*

Today is another morning of independence for me as a consultant. Wouldn't you like to be one, too?

Businesses have traditionally hired consultants in standard areas like human resources, technology, public relations, marketing, legal, and finance. Today, however, businesses seek out consultants and other Independents in nearly any specialty you can think of—from video production to managing municipal waste plants. Industrial agriculture, logistics, contact centers ... If it's a specialty, you can become an expert consultant!

For most of my career, I have been that guy working from home, working from a beach, and (usually) taking vacations to other places when I want. For more than fifteen years, I've lived the highs and lows of the Independent life and defined myself through it. I have worked very hard, made some mistakes, and learned much along the way. And that's just the business side of it: in that same time, I've gone from being single in Brooklyn to being married in the 'burbs with three young children. My wife and I have gone through the inevitable challenges of caring for aging parents. Through it all, I have been an independent consultant and have grown my annual revenues (my salary, more or less) by an average of 25 percent per year.

The most important lesson that I've learned is that consulting is more than a *job*—it's a *lifestyle*. Today, I work as a free man. I'm Independent. And even on my worst days "at work," I am grateful for the freedom I have.

I want to share what I have learned with you because I believe that most of us need help in achieving career and life success under the ebb and flow of our modern economic conditions. Whatever you're going through, chances are I've been there, and I'm here to help. I've worked with a big range of clients, from mom-and-pop businesses to global corporations, and my best practices are designed to help you work—and live—under a variety of business and personal conditions.

The pages ahead. I have written this book for you. Here's what you can expect:

1. A concise look at why *now* is the right time for you to take the big step and Transition to Independence

2. A process that will help you to distill your particular expertise into a marketable asset that you feel good about

3. Guidance to help you understand what the Independent lifestyle is like and how to prepare yourself and those in your life for these changes

4. A low-risk transition plan that will allow you to repeatedly test the waters of Independence

5. Broad-ranging advice on how to take your expertise and elevate yourself into a better consultant—improving earning potential and your ability to get beyond *work* and into *life*

You can be one of the winners. If you are able to follow the steps I have outlined in this book, you can make at least as much money as you are making now (and quite possibly much more) while working in a happier environment and creating more time for life. You can be on a career path that is open to new opportunities for more income and creative satisfaction. When you're in the groove, this becomes a virtuous cycle of happy client / enhanced skills and experience / increased earning potential for future projects.

If you are ready to get started, grab an empty beach chair and sit with me for a while. The weather is wonderful, and the forecast is sunny and warm for days and days to come.

—Aaron Zwas

CHAPTER 1

Three Reasons Why Today Should Be Your Independence Day

Ironically, from a professional person's point of view, freedom is just another word for working for yourself. So, not surprisingly, consultants—by definition "people who provide expert advice professionally"—are growing in number as a natural result of the shifting tides of our modern economy.

As you can imagine, I discuss the topic of Independence often. I usually receive feedback along the lines of, "I don't work from the beach like you, but at least I've got a stable income and healthcare. Why take the risk of going Independent?" It's a fair question that deserves an answer at the outset of this book.

As with many of life's big decisions, there is the money response and the personal response. And the closer you examine these responses, the more sense the Transition to Independence makes.

REASON #1: YOUR WHITE-COLLAR JOB IS BECOMING A COMMODITY

Chances are that your career stability is less solid than you'd like to believe. Big macro-economic trends are fundamentally changing how we work, and it's no longer your father's job market out there. These changes are coming quickly, and they will be here to stay.

Job migration. The first trend is a no-brainer that has been at play for several decades now: the migration of American (and other traditional Western economies') jobs into the global job market— first, with manufacturing (Japan, Korea, China, Mexico), then with services (call centers in Canada, the Philippines), and now with positions like technology consulting (India). Quite simply, this trend, which has put blue-collar work at risk for a generation, has now encroached into white-collar work.

Turning ideas into money. The second trend is a result of the first: as these jobs become commoditized, it drives mature economies to advance toward ideas. Almost since its inception, America has been, and remains, at the vanguard of "The Idea Economy"— where fresh ideas (innovations, inventions, refinements) are highly valued and aggressively pursued. The growth of this trend is very real, and it favors independent consultants who are able to clearly articulate their expertise and use it to deliver value to their clients.

It's how employers want it to be. The third factor may have the most profound effect on your career: employers are driving the trend toward consulting and independent work, regardless of your thoughts on the topic. Labor is, in effect, becoming a utility. Like water and electricity, employers can increasingly turn the faucet for more or less talent as they need it. According to the *Forbes* magazine 2013 article, "How an Exploding Freelance Economy Will Drive Change in 2014," :

> *Talent is moving from a fixed cost (and one that's historically been one of the largest across a business) to a variable cost, with companies staffing up and down as needed. Businesses have the ability to quickly on-board hundreds ... of freelance workers ... We see no signs of that [trend] slowing down in 2014 and beyond.*

Simply put, employers are able to minimize their hefty labor costs by shifting from full-time employees to a sizable mix of Independents (including contractors). This allows employers to effectively pay as they go for expertise and manpower when they need it only. They find further efficiencies because they don't have to pay for healthcare, bonuses, or other auxiliary costs for Independents. Throw in the growing acceptance of remote workers, and employers' expenses shrink even more by eliminating the need for actual office space.

This is *your* career, your job, we're talking about here. If you don't get ahead of these trends, you'll easily become a victim of them—living with less certainty, safety, and control over your income and quality of work and life.

> If you don't get ahead of these trends, you'll easily become a victim of them

The Transition to Independence provides a method through these treacherous waters by helping you in two primary areas:

- distilling and articulating your current skills into an expertise so that you stand out as an expert thinker in a global crowd of lower-priced doers
- sharing game plans for transitioning to, and thriving within, the inherently more dynamic world of independent consulting

REASON #2: YOU ARE NOT HAPPY

It's likely that you've bought this book because you're somehow unhappy, dissatisfied, frustrated, or exhausted. Perhaps you feel like you're being held back or that you have no control of your career, and it's stopping you from living life on your own terms.

I know what that's like. I've been there.

Let me share a quick story on where I started out and how I came to write this book.

My Spanish step. My first job out of college that didn't involve a cash register was as a technical writer at a computer-software company in Ithaca, NY. The job, overall, was a satisfying start to "real life," but after about a year and a half into it, an unexpected opportunity presented itself to me: a friend in New York City asked if I would like to travel to Spain for two months and write for a travel guide.

I was ecstatic. My friend had called because she knew that I had been trying to get back to Spain ever since I had spent a college semester abroad a few years earlier, and this opportunity would help build my credentials as a fledgling professional writer. I would be paid to travel around in Spain for two months and write about it! Paid!

To further sweeten the deal, I decided that I would follow several of my friends and move to New York City upon my return. The assignment started in a month. I was twenty-five years old and without serious attachments. A great adventure and my life's next chapter awaited me.

But here's where it gets interesting. *I almost didn't go.*

While the *experience* of the Spain gig was definitely going to be awesome, the *paid* part was really just enough for me to break even while I travelled. I was still heavily in debt from college, and getting started in New York City was going to be expensive. The "adult" decision was obvious: keep my corporate job in Ithaca, save money much faster, and *then* move to New York City.

Big decisions always involve change. I was on the brink of turning down the opportunity of a lifetime when, three days later, I got another lucky break via a friend who was a manager at work. "We are going to be working on a distance-learning program in the fall," she told me. "Didn't you study some of that in school? We just need some help in getting it started for a couple months. Maybe you could do that for us as a consultant, after Spain?"

That was the magic formula: *consultant*. Everything instantly fell into place. She would hire me as a specialist after my trip. The money would be enough to pay my loans *and* see me off to New York a few 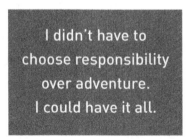 months later. Plus I would be able to add a new professional skill set to my youthful résumé. I didn't have to choose responsibility over adventure. I could have it all.

And so my career as an Independent was born.

The deal could not have worked out better. By the end of that year, I had completed my first consulting engagement, been published in a travel guide to Europe, and found myself a new position at a boutique consulting firm in New York City.

Once there, I honed many of the hard skills related to my particular brand of consulting and was fortunate enough to be exposed to the value of what we then called "teleworking." My employer had no corporate office. Formal company meetings were held in a rented space in Midtown, and we did the rest by phone or ad-hoc at client sites and restaurants. I could tell you that I "worked from home," which is true—but I also worked from coffee shops, my parents' house during extended visits, and most notably from a beach house in Montauk, Long Island, for the better part of the summer of 2001. My productivity never waned.

This open structure was accommodating enough, in fact, that I pursued another travel-writing venture in 2002. Instead of Spain, however, this journey took me to Ireland. The small country qualified for the FIFA World Cup soccer finals that year, and although the tournament itself was being co-hosted by Japan and Korea, I thought it

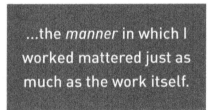

...the *manner* in which I worked mattered just as much as the work itself.

would be great fun to be in Ireland during the three-week adventure that would surely absorb the entire sports-fanatic nation.

I arranged a leave of absence with my employer, during which I took no pay. But I did sell an article to a small American soccer magazine. The compensation again covered all of my travel expenses, Ireland fully delivered an adventure to me, and my appreciation for Independence continued to grow.

My Irish sweepstakes. After the Ireland trip, I was starting to get it: the *manner* in which I worked mattered just as much as the work itself. I could do this over and over, if I chose to do so. Six months later, I set up a website, filed some legal paperwork, and committed fully to my new lifestyle. In the decade since then, I have adopted, evolved, and have now codified my knowledge into the Transition to Independence (T2I) plan.

The point is that I've lived through the transition I'm selling you. I came to realize that Independence allows a person to pursue his or her passions—whatever they might be—and still pay the rent.

REASON #3: THERE HAS NEVER BEEN A BETTER TIME

My first two reasons for transitioning to Independence are borne out of challenges to overcome. Reason number three is easy: at no time in history has the barrier to entry for a new business been lower! As an independent consultant, you will not need a physical store, inventory, or employees.  All in all, the cost of running my consultancy out of my home ranges from two thousand to five thousand dollars a year (I hit the high end of that range when I buy a new laptop every three years or create a new website every five). My profit margin never dips below 90 percent. I still have to pay my own healthcare, but still, no matter how you slice it, any other business opportunity that costs less is probably a pyramid scheme.

You are your own MVP. And cost is only half the equation. The other half is what I like to call "The Team of One." Our digital and connected world creates the opportunity for an individual—you—

to produce much of the work that once required an entire team. Specialists are waiting to help you with the rest. Web designers, virtual assistants, social-media experts, logo designers, researchers, and almost anyone else you could need to start and maintain your business are out there at reasonable per-hour rates. Combine these specialists with the simple technologies that we now take for granted—like color printers, video chat, and desktop-publishing applications—and you can now accomplish on your own as much as a small team could accomplish twenty years ago.

And, of course, the whole world is now your sales region. Yes, this can work against you too (see Reason #1, above), but—with the right positioning of your expertise—you can use this dynamic to your advantage. From my home near the shores of New Jersey, I have worked with clients in New York City, Dallas, Florida, San Francisco, Las Vegas, Boston, Puerto Rico, England, Germany, France, Spain, and Hong Kong.

• • •

So even if you're not sold on working from the beach, I hope you will agree with me that the Transition to Independence is not really a question of *if*, but *when*. There is no doubt that there are real challenges and risks on the horizon, but there are unique opportunities, too.

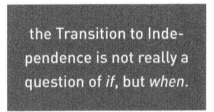
the Transition to Independence is not really a question of *if*, but *when*.

THE T2I PLAN

This plan is crucial to understanding my book. T2I means Transition to Independence. Very specifically, the plan helps you find your way to happiness by:

- sharing advice on how to *live the lifestyle* and not just *work*
- communicating the lifestyle vision to your family and friends and bringing them along for the ride
- opening a community to help you make the transition and then to continually elevate your game

The diagram above is a visual table of contents for this book. We will refer back to this diagram at the top of each chapter to help keep you oriented and focused on completing *your* Transition to Independence. We will also refer often to this book's accompanying website— www.t2iplan.com—which contains deeper dives on selected topics, templates, and the T2I community for sharing experiences on transitioning to, and living in, Independence.

With the T2I Plan and the T2I community, you will have what you need to live the life you want, and it's never been easier! These changes are coming, regardless of your perspective. Make the most of it!

CHAPTER 2

Consulting Is Right for You

I have been training client-side employees to think and work like consultants for over a decade, so trust me on this: nothing in this book will have anything to do with your age, your gender, specific job titles, or specific academic degrees (specialized cases aside). I can say with confidence that most of us can do this work—regardless of our specific domain of expertise.

The main thing is a small thing. The prolific film director Woody Allen once said, "80 percent of success is showing up," and I count that as "showing up with an intent to do a great job." The key factor in determining your success in this line of work is a commitment to quality and excellence. If you can really tune into that, really commit to it, nearly everything else that we will discuss is plain old blocking and tackling— basic stuff. To that end, we will be focusing a lot on the qualitative side of consulting. Doing so creates the best opportunity for you to live independently and also offers your potential clients the best possible value.

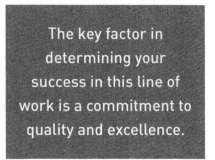

The key factor in determining your success in this line of work is a commitment to quality and excellence.

So what, exactly, is a consultant? I'm glad you asked …

• • •

Some people might define "consultant" as "someone on a mobile phone keeping Starbucks in business." However, if you are going to be a *successful* consultant, it's probably better to define this term from the client's point of view. It's a nuanced shift but one that has tremendous importance in determining your success.

Become part of the home team. To illustrate, let's imagine a project for creating a new product is being proposed: a subscription-only industry-analysis newsletter. The team gathers in the office of the vice president of e-commerce to discuss. As they talk through the effort, they begin to realize that it will need input from many teams, including editorial, marketing, technology, and even the contact center. They begin to understand that they can't just dump this on the new website-content gal.

Someone says, "I think we need a consultant for this. I don't have the extra resources to manage a big project like this." A second person adds, "And even if we did, I don't think we have the in-house knowledge to distribute successfully." The executive, who has been listening quietly as the discussion has grown, now leans forward. "Why?" she asks. "What, specifically, would a consultant do for us that we cannot do on our own?"

This is the crucial moment.

Nine times out of ten the answer will focus on the Five Client-Value Points I've included on the following pages. These points do not focus on the specifics of an actual specialty; they are designed to apply to any sort of consulting, from aerospace engineering to social-media content.

The Five Client Value Points. These are the benefits you will bring to the table. Know them well, and don't be afraid to spell them out.

1. **Expertise:** Your client will *gain value* from your knowledge—usually because the client does not have your degree of knowledge and experience in-house. See chapter 8 for more on how to best define and market your expertise.

2. **Quality:** Perhaps because they have not transitioned to Independence, at least two-thirds of the people in most companies are phoning it in. They don't care about excellence. They don't care about quality. But you do! Clients *gain value* from your work when it is thorough, thoughtful, professional, timely, and re-useable. They also gain value when their employees improve the quality of their work based on your lead. Sometimes this is an explicit component of a consultant's work, but I have seen many examples of this value being realized passively, too. See chapter 7 for more.

3. **Time to Focus:** In modern lean and fast-moving organizations, many clients *gain value* from someone who has the undistracted bandwidth (that is, time and head space) to keep things on track and moving according to schedule. They also gain value by having someone *thinking* on their behalf. Most employees, with their stacks of daily responsibilities, just don't have the time to ponder questions like "What is the competition doing?" or "How can we manage this process more efficiently?" When done correctly, you can be in the enviable position of being a brain-for-hire by simply asking and pursuing questions like these.

4. **An Outsider's View:** Even the most enlightened organizations run into challenges as a result of (1) stale or insular strategic

thinking (a.k.a. groupthink) or (2) incomplete strategy/ planning that accounts for one team but not another (a.k.a. silos). Because consultants are outsiders, we are inherently liberated from these mental constraints. Clients *gain value* when you share the best possible solution to a problem (impartial to department lines) and fresh thinking that draws in outside views and/or cross-team inputs. We'll talk about these more in chapter 7, too.

5. **The Long View**: Good consultants look for client opportunities that are related to their original assignment. Examples can include opportunities for improvement and can also include more blue-sky opportunities, like a potentially underserved market need. Clients *gain value* by being made aware of such opportunities—whether they elect to pursue them or not. As a bonus, this type of value helps clients to understand how else you might help them down the road. There's plenty more to discuss on this topic. See chapter 7 for more.

So forget what the dictionary tells you. Expertise, quality, focus, outsider's view, and the long view. *That's* what a consultant provides. *That's* why any organization would ever bother with you. And *that's* the mind-set you need to be successful! I still refer to these points on a regular basis when I'm assessing how well I'm doing with my clients and/or prospects.

Commit to quality. So, I encourage you to get comfortable with the five client-value points. Pay attention to the fact that only the first of these points, expertise, is something specialized. It's the other four points that I've trained so many people on over the years. Take to heart how much they matter, and understand that you are capable of that level of quality. Commit to quality, and you're well on your way!

Related to that first value point, let's move on to the next chapter. We will get out of the theoretical and get hands-on with defining *you* as a consultant so that you are able to clearly state the benefit you bring to potential clients and market yourself appropriately.

CHAPTER 3

Step 1: Define Your Consulting Expertise

In this chapter, we will roll up our sleeves and begin to work through the first steps of the Transition to Independence plan. The T2I Plan will help you create a sustainable independent career that enables you to work and live on *your* terms, without having to sacrifice your income.

The first part of the T2I Plan is called **Define your Consulting Expertise (DiCE)**. This is a process that will help you to distill and define *your* expertise into an easily understood and marketable service.

> define *your* expertise into an easily understood and marketable service.

Leave nothing to chance. These plans are built directly from my own consulting experiences. In various forms, I've been a consultant since 1999, during which time I have interacted with a broad set of professionals within my clients' organizations. I listen to their stories, I come to understand the nature of their work, and I gain insight into how they provide value to their organizations and how to make the most of it. As part of my particular type of consulting, I have had such conversations with many people over the course of my career.

I have cross-referenced this body of knowledge with the emerging form of the Idea Economy to create the Define Your Consulting Expertise plan. DiCE comprises six steps that can take anywhere from a few days to several weeks to complete. The *right* amount of time depends on your current state of affairs and the urgency with which you want to begin the next chapter of your life. If you can find two or three evenings a week to work on your DiCE, you should be able to complete it in about two to four weeks.

> **How to play DiCE like a high roller.** Here are the parts:
>
> 1. Create Your Expertise Sketch
> 2. Define Your Value-Add
> 3. Create Your New Title and Description
> 4. Define Your Market
> 5. Get a Life
>
> Each of these are mini-projects in their own right. You should expect to need a few sessions for each of the five parts in the DiCE plan. To help keep you on track, you can download a checklist and samples at t2iplan.com.

PART 1: CREATE YOUR EXPERTISE SKETCH

Our strategy is to transform the experiences of your current career into a marketable consulting expertise. (Important note: if you are looking to start a new line of work entirely, that's more of an entrepreneurial endeavor, which I am not covering in this book.) So with that in mind, grab your current résumé, some additional paper, and a pen. Find a quiet place and give yourself at least two hours at a time for this activity. Each of these steps should occur on its own piece of paper. And do try to stick with pen and paper at this point; laptops (and other devices) offer too many distractions ... (Note: If you would prefer a simple template instead of the blank-slate approach, you can find one at t2iplan.com).

HOW TO MAKE A WINNING GAME PLAN

Step 1: Update your current résumé. Include your current and previous job titles (distribution manager, HR specialist, etc.). Take time to define (with bullet points) your primary responsibilities. Note: You don't need a polished look here. These updates are for your eyes only.

Step 2: Write down the standard set of business processes that you participate in. This is the what-you-do step, and it may overlap with the responsibilities you listed in your previous step. *Be specific.* Think about the work you do day-to-day, at month end, and at year end. Also list responsibilities related to what counts as a *special event* in your line of work. Examples include new clients, new services, new websites going live, or perhaps when new stores are opened.

Step 3: Jot down the metrics that you measure in your job. By what metrics is your work currently judged? Are there other metrics you'd like to add to the list? If yes, go for it. List healthy and dangerous values for each metric and define what counts as *success*. Examples of these metrics can vary widely, depending on the nature of your current work. As a general guideline, focus on metrics related to time, money, and errors/issues.

Step 4: Make a list of common challenges. Keep this list specific to the job itself. (Example: Do NOT include things like "I hate working with Bill in Accounting.") In addition to the challenges that you face, think about your whole team—department and manager. What challenges/issues does he or she face? Add them to the list. Examples might include onboarding new clients, customer service for foreign customers, or a dwindling consumer market. Again, the items in this list will vary substantially based on your work.

Step 5: Describe how to do that work better (more efficiently, with better quality, etc.). Make a list of what you know works—either because you've seen it in action or because you've been around long enough to know what would be best. Make sure you include something here that would address each of the points you listed in the prior step.

Step 6: Write down anything else that is related to the success of your work but not controlled by your team. As an example, I often reach out to the client's call center when discussing websites because call center agents often use the same website as customers to help understand what they are looking at. Does your success depend on successful transitions with other teams or other external factors? List the teams, external factors, and your connection to them here.

Step 7: List the different types of businesses you have worked in or could work in. What industry do you know the best? Have you worked in small businesses? Big ones? Non-profits? Manufacturing? Pull this right from your résumé. Add to it as feels comfortable.

Congratulations, you've just assembled a first-draft outline of your DiCE document! If you conducted the exercise correctly, you should have a relatively succinct codification of your work expertise. It might not look like much yet, but it will. That small stack of papers is the raw material that we will build with in the coming chapters.

Once you've completed the first draft of "Your Expertise Sketch," go through the following additional activities.

- **Let the work sit for a day or two**. Then revisit and revise.
- **Take your time**, and take two or three passes (revisions) at it. Be thorough.
- **Type up your DiCE document** in any electronic format that works for you—but only after you are satisfied with your handwritten drafts

A consulting plan

To see an example of a DiCE plan at this stage, go to www.t2iplan.com.

Before you turn the page ... I'd like to address two common concerns I see at this point:

- **Don't be a person who downplays what you know.** What is mundane and obvious to one person is truly *specialized knowledge* to someone else. You have years of details and experiences in your head. Believe in your expertise!
- **Don't try too hard.** If you feel like your list is too small or not deep enough, don't worry. You have to start somewhere. In the later chapters of this book, I will show you how you can evolve your expertise over time with increasingly sophisticated clients and assignments.

PART 2: DEFINE YOUR VALUE-ADD

In chapter 2, we defined the Five Client Value Points. This concept of *value-add* is core to all types of consulting. Whereas most people describe what they do when you ask them about work, good consultants always respond with the *value they create*—also known as their value-add. This subtle but important shift keeps you focused on answering the simple question that any potential client would ask: "Why should I hire you?"

> **Why should they hire you?** Let's say you're an e-commerce expert. At some point, you will need to answer that important if obvious question. It's one likely to be asked one way or another, by most potential clients, so here's a short cheat-sheet to use by way of example:
>
> - **Traditional employee:** I am an e-commerce analyst. I build and run reports related to our website and apps. About once a quarter, I add those numbers to data from other areas like the contact center and our retail outlets for our executive team.
> - **E-commerce consultant:** I help to *identify opportunities for revenue growth* and to measure the *effectiveness of new strategies/ campaigns* via digital channels by building the necessary reports.
>
> Who would you rather hire as a specialist? The difference is clear, right?

Fortunately, the art of defining value-add is simple. First, let's return to your expertise sketch from pages 29-30. Looking at the steps in "How to Make a Winning Game Plan" in part 1, our impulse might be to dwell on step 2 "What You Do," but we now understand that the value-add content is really under "Metrics" in step 3, where you describe the *results* of that work. These results, the output of your work, are the value-add, and this is all that matters. If you're not adding value as a consultant, you're not doing your job.

To answer the "Why should I hire you?" question, part 2 focuses on writing bullet points that summarize the metrics in your expertise

> If you're not adding value as a consultant, you're not doing your job.

sketch. You should begin to come up with responses like…

- increase revenue
- reduce cost
- improve brand equity
- improve efficiency
- improve moral
- become compliant with…

As you go through this step, do *not* attempt to assign a value-add to each metric in your expertise sketch. Zoom out a bit. Synthesize. Imagine looking down on your area of expertise from above. This *manager's view* or *executive's view* will help you to put your work into the context of the bigger picture so that you can discuss your value-add more easily.

When ready, write down (or type up) your value-add statement under "Value-Add" in your Transition to Independence plan. When you are done, you should have a simple statement like the example above. One or two sentences is enough, and your statement should be easily understood by experts and laymen alike.

As with the prior step (your DiCE plan), take your time and go through a few drafts. And as always, see t2iplan.com if you're looking for feedback or additional examples.

PART 3: CREATE YOUR NEW TITLE AND DESCRIPTION

The title and description that you choose for yourself will have an impact on your success as a consultant. If your description is short and simple enough, it will improve your ability to sell yourself. And, it will help others to connect you with the right potential clients. I have found that many people are willing to help make connections and introductions, but they have to understand what you do in order for those efforts to be helpful!

How to make yourself crystal clear.
If you tell new acquaintances that you "analyze clients and share best practices for defining an optimized set of standard operating procedures," very few people will know what to do with that. Instead, here are a few clear and positive examples:

- I consult with local non-profits to help them increase donations by using email direct marketing.
- I advise on best practices for e-commerce solutions like websites and mobile apps. I typically work with the chief marketing officer of midsized corporations who do a lot of e-commerce business.
- I am a training specialist. I typically work with franchise companies who are rolling out new technologies and processes to their franchise owners.

Creating succinct descriptions like these is relatively simple, once you have the right raw materials. Fortunately, that's exactly what we've been working on in the prior two parts of this chapter. Use that material in this formula:

**I [value-add] for [businesses I have worked with]
by [summary of what I do]**

"Value-add" is from part 2 of your DiCE plan,
"Business I have worked with" is step 7 in your expertise sketch, and
"Summary of what you do" is informed by step 2 in your expertise sketch.

Words you'll live by. Your description will become the cornerstone of the collateral materials that you will be building in the following chapters, including your website and your LinkedIn profile.

> If your description is short and simple enough, it will improve your ability to sell yourself.

Remember your self-description has to be short and simple enough for others to explain it on your behalf if they are making a referral. Spend time working on this and try to boil it down to the bare minimum of what a potential client would need to know. Don't make it an elevator speech. Make it a single-step speech. I've been through this process personally more than once, and here are some tactics that have worked for me:

- Write out different versions and try them on for size.
- Run your preferred descriptions by trusted friends for feedback.
- Google your phrase and see if the results seem congruent with what you are attempting to offer or to see if it's been used so often that it's trite (or worse, is somebody else's proprietary language!).

Don't get obsessive! A word of caution on this step: Many people, myself included, are tempted to spend days and weeks on this exercise. Just remember that everyone else in the world will dwell on your description for two to three seconds before moving on to their next thought! So spend time to get it right, but be reasonable and remember that you can always change your description as your work evolves.

PART 4: DEFINE YOUR MARKET

The focus of this part is to define who would be interested in your expertise so that you can tailor a better message for them.

In step 7 of your expertise sketch, you defined the different types of businesses and regions in which you have worked. That list is a starting point for identifying people who might hire you in the future. So let's review it and try to amplify it. Consider customers of your current employer. Consider, also, if there are particular business scenarios where your skills would be useful. Examples could include "expanding into Latin American markets," or "seeking to merge a recently acquired business," or "must comply with new regulations." Think again about the *executive's view* or the *manager's view*. What business scenarios would they be considering?

When you're done with this activity, you should have a good first draft of types of businesses that would gain value from your skill set. Now is also a good time to review your work in parts 2 and 3 and make any refinements that might be helpful.

PART 5: GET A LIFE

We now have a great rough sketch of what you, as a consultant, will look like to others: your title, your value-add description, a résumé of prior experiences, and who might be looking for you.

Define your expertise via creating foundational marketing materials.

What you want to do next is to put these into a format that someone else would want to read. That format is usually a bio, and it can serve as the cornerstone for two very basic marketing tools: LinkedIn and your website. Depending on the nature of your consulting, one or more social-media channels may also act as primary channels; a bio can be useful there, too.

Your professional bio is a long-form version of your value-add statement, mixed in with some résumé-level detail and a little bit of personality. For example, my bio mentions that I live in New Jersey with my young family and that I'm a pinball enthusiast.

Bio note: The feel is more like a very, very short story. Just like the prior activities in our T2I Plan, you'll want to write a few versions, let it sit for a few days, and then try again. Here are a few best practices for bios to keep in mind as you work on yours:

- Refer to yourself in the third person.
- Bios are great for sharing a little more personality—words like passion, commitment, and dedication are all welcome here.
- Including a few sentences about yourself is great: where you live, any hobbies, etc. ...
- A little showmanship is okay in a bio.
- Anywhere from 150 to about 450 words is a good length, but remember, a typical piece of typing paper, comfortably formatted, should contain no more than 250 words. So you might want to make that your limit. A personal bio that goes on for more than one page may be TMI (too much information) for busy readers.

If this style of writing is not your forte, you can rely on fellow freelancers to assist. A simple post to TaskRabbit, Upwork, or Craigslist will get you in touch with someone who can help. And, as always, you can see examples and find support at t2iplan.com.

Create your first-draft website.

As you work on your bio, you should also begin to work on the first-draft version of your website. Your website, we all know, is the primary method by which people will discover and/or learn more about you. Many Independents don't realize, however, that the *creation* of your website—the actual process of deciding what it will say—is a very effective method for further defining your services and value-add. It is for this reason that you are starting with a draft version of your website at this early point in the T2I Plan.

Unlike even a few years ago, great-looking websites are now inexpensive (or free) and very easy to build. Because you are going to start with a draft website, create a free account with one of the great new website platforms like Weebly or Squarespace. Don't worry about a website domain (the part after "www.") yet. It can wait until we talk more about branding in chapter 4.

All you need to know about webpage design. A modern website for consultants need not be bloated with pages of services and helpful links or interactive apps. As a consultant, the primary goals of your website are:
to clearly state the services you offer and the value-add of those services
to convey a suitably respectable and professional image
to help interested parties contact you

With that in mind, I recommend a simple three-page approach:
1. Home page: Include your name and your title (additional tag line optional). Then add additional detail about the specifics of what you offer (from parts 2 and 3 of this chapter), but include no more than a paragraph or two.
2. About page: This is your professional bio (from page 37 of this part, above).
3. Contact page: Include email, phone, relevant social channels, and office address (aka your home address).

For the first two pages, you might also consider get-in-touch-to-learn-more links that lead to the contact page. If you have an inclination for this sort of thing, by all means play with the format. Some people find that a single page does the job, for example. Just keep in mind that online, less is more. Remember to keep your message simple and direct so that it is easily understood by the broadest appropriate audience.

Regardless of the format, remember that your website is still in draft format at this time. No one else will know that it is there. Experiment. Play with the text. Seek input. Then walk away for a few days. When you are done with this step, you should be looking at a website that has no logo but a good first-draft structure that you can build upon in the next chapters.

Create (but don't yet publish) your updated LinkedIn profile.

I do not recommend that you publish an updated LinkedIn profile yet, but it is a good time to create that content based on our work in this chapter. The LinkedIn summary should be your value-add statement, and your experience should be updated based on your revised résumé. If you find it helpful, save this in a distinct word-processing document for later reference.

> **You are here.** If you've been able to go through my DiCE system for defining your consulting expertise, you should now have the following:
> 1. Your title and concise description
> 2. Your simple value-add statement
> 3. A professional bio (and, in your back pocket, an updated résumé)
> 4. A list of potential client types and scenarios
> 5. A succinct first-draft website (which we will evolve in the next chapter)
> 6. A sense of confidence in how much you have accomplished

Once you have reached this point, I recommend that you pause for a few days and then review the materials again with a fresh mind. Make any refinements that you might find helpful. And then? Do something nice for yourself. You've achieved a big victory simply by getting this far! You will use all of these materials in the next chapter, and they should serve you far beyond the activities described in this book.

CHAPTER 4

Step 2: Create Your Prep Plan

You should now have a healthy first draft of your DiCE Plan, which is the cornerstone of your overall Transition to Independence. If your plan has turned out well, you should have a much sharper vision of what you would look like as an independent consultant, and, therefore, the confidence to move on to our next set of activities: the "Prep Plan."

The combination of working remotely and working independently form an experience that is fundamentally different from traditional office work. The Prep Plan helps you to transition into this different experience by sharing insights into the day-to-day living of Independence and a blueprint for preparing and optimizing the primary dynamics of it. If you think of your DiCE Plan as your egg, the Prep Plan is the nest—and you want that nest to be a healthy environment that fosters the greatest chances for your success.

THE PREP PLAN

The Prep Plan comprises five simple but important parts:
1. Prepare Yourself
2. Prepare Your Family and Friends
3. Prepare Your Organization
4. Prepare Your Brand
5. Prepare Your Workspace

After you complete these parts, you will have a solid foundation from which you can begin selling yourself as a consultant and taking on your first clients—both of which we will cover later.

PART 1: PREPARE YOURSELF

When I transitioned to Independence, I did so without enough help and guidance. Yes, I experienced the highlights of traveling and writing, but I didn't understand, really, what I was getting into. On many occasions, I questioned the path I was taking. But my experience and lessons learned grew as time went by. I came to understand the inherent characteristics of the independent-consulting experience, and as my knowledge grew, it became much easier for me to stress less and succeed more.

Now, I am sharing my lessons with you so that you can make the transition and live the Independent lifestyle without going through the same pain points that I did.

Reality check. Lessons learned aside, however, you still need a reality check: much like riding a bike, I assure you that you will fall and get a few bruises during this transition. Economic highs and lows will pass; friends and family might not offer the initial support you're seeking, and potential clients might behave in erratic ways. Through it all, your best hope at success and ultimate happiness is by honing in on yourself. This "Prepare Yourself" section focuses on that; it's about developing the fortitude and flexibility that you'll need to get back on the bike and try again.

Prepare Yourself Financially

The Transition to Independence will almost certainly require you to temporarily dip into savings. So just to be clear and to keep yourself safe: I do NOT recommend the T2I Plan if you're looking to make more money in the short term.

What to Expect:

Even after you make a full Transition to Independence, you should expect that your ongoing cash flow will be less dependable than standard employment. Most independent consultants are like farmers—we either get a lot of rain and a good crop or get a drought and very little crop. While I can certainly influence my pipeline more than I can the clouds, macroeconomic conditions can convene, like the housing-market crash in 2008, to make life very challenging. And even in good times, work can dissipate quickly because of unforeseen circumstances and misunderstandings.

Start with a plan. I encourage you to take every precaution when preparing yourself financially. Develop a plan that helps to minimize risk related to your transition period but also one that will be able to handle the inherent highs and lows of independent consulting. To prepare yourself adequately, I recommend...

- **Hire brains.** If you have an accountant, have a private exploratory conversation with him or her.
- **Review your monthly budget.** I am surprised by how cavalier some people can be with this. Do not be one of those people. Even if you're on a budget already, now is a great time to see if you can dial things down for the next six months. Hold off on any big expenses, if possible.
- **Have a year in the bank** before formally ending your full-time employment. If you are able to manage it, build up enough savings to get you through one year of standard expenses. This is true even if you "have something lined up" or other informal agreements.

One final note on this topic: Creating sound financial plans and habits up front creates some protection from ongoing thoughts and worries about money. This, in turn, will help to keep your head focused on making the transition and improving your work—instead of constantly worrying about your wallet.

Prepare Yourself Mentally (and Yes, Physically)

The transition from a traditional career to independent consulting is full of subtle changes that can add up to a powerful wallop if you're not prepared. I've seen many people get sucker punched by the one-two combination of (1) having *all* aspects of the job depend on you, and (2) dealing with this unexpected workload in relative isolation.

While some newly minted Independents are an immediate success in this new environment, the result for many people is a loss of time and morale or just an overall degradation of joy in their work and personal lives. I have fallen into all of these traps, and I had to dig my way back out. By becoming familiar with them in advance and preparing yourself accordingly, you can avoid that same fate and get to Independence that much more quickly.

What to Expect:

There are two things you should anticipate happening once you declare your independence:

First, you will be the entire organization. In addition to providing your expertise for hire, you will become the vice president of sales and the CEO. You'll also be the vice president of marketing. And the administrative assistant. And the ... well, you get the idea. As an independent consultant, be prepared to spend more time than anticipated on activities *not* directly related to providing professional advice or services for a fee. Of particular note …

You will become a salesperson. Salespeople are usually a special breed, and you're about to become one of them. After all, your consultancy isn't going to sell itself! This task is hard enough for many of us in general, and the stress factor will only go up when the product you're selling is YOU.

You will become your own boss. Great! Right? Well, usually. But, just like people benefit from a personal trainer to help them get to the gym, there are benefits to having someone else around to keep you accountable. When you're on your own, you are the first and last line of defense in ensuring that your clients receive the attention and quality that exceeds their expectations. We usually frame this absence of oversight as liberating, but it often becomes an enormous challenge that new Independents have to work through.

Second, there is going to be a lot more *you* in your life. You will define yourself through your business: when you have a "normal job," there is a natural separation between your work and, well, you. When you go independent, however, *you* are the service being sold, and the success (or potential failure) of selling that service falls squarely on *your* shoulders. When you add the fact that you are the entire organization (see above), the resulting experience tends to be a merging of your self-identity and your job. This shift in your personal identity is no small thing. Most Independents don't even realize it is happening to them (I didn't), even as they create growing pressure and task lists for themselves. If you really want to make the most of your independence, you must go into this transformation with specific mental boundaries between *you* and *work*.

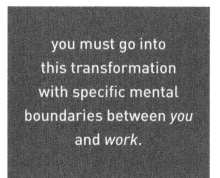

you must go into this transformation with specific mental boundaries between *you* and *work*.

You will be more isolated than in your current job. Finally, as you go through all of the personal changes I describe here, you'll be doing so in relative isolation. And once you complete your transition? You'll still be isolated—it's just part of the job. I always tell people: you better know who your friends are before you start working from home, because you won't be bumping into new people padding around your house with a laptop!

LONELY HEARTS NOTES:

Don't act like a loner. In addition to the loss of camaraderie, it is much harder, too, to pick up on social queues when you work remotely. Did that phone call not go well because the client is genuinely unhappy with the work or because he or she is just having a bad day? It can be hard to tell from a distance.

Lean on friends for conversation. When we add in the significant amount of change that come along with the transition, many new Independents find that they are taking on a lot more, mentally and emotionally, than anticipated—and with fewer natural outlets like office colleagues, to boot. A regular lunch routine can help here, and so can social activities, like clubs, groups, etc.

Additional workload, more stress, and loneliness: Doesn't exactly sound like a joyful life experience, right? On the contrary, these challenges are surmountable and very much worth the effort. All you need is a little guidance from someone, like me, who's been through this before. And remember why you are reading this book—you should be excited! You're on a path that will enable you to live and work on your terms.

THINK AHEAD.

Preparing yourself mentally is one of the most significant elements of independent consulting and also one of the most underestimated. When you're successful, you will feel on top of the world, but when you hit challenging times, it is very easy to put a lot of negativity on yourself. It can cut deep. In order to be successful and really achieve Independence, you need to keep your head in the game!

Your number-one best bet for preparing yourself mentally is to progress on the lifestyle elements of Independence alongside the specific work details. Going into this with a healthy balance of nonwork activity can help you to keep your eye on the prize, reduce stress, and keep your self-identity spread across more than the wins and losses of your career. If that weren't enough, research shows that taking time for nonwork activi-

...research shows that taking time for nonwork activities helps you to be more efficient when you do work.

ties helps you to be more efficient when you do work. So, don't use "I've got too much to do" as an excuse to avoid these steps—you'll be shortchanging the quality of your work *and* the quality of your life.

My recommendations for preparing yourself mentally:

Trade "solitary confinement" for "public isolation." Working solo doesn't mean you have to be physically alone. Working in a shared office space can be a great way to recreate many of the social dynamics of the workplace that you would otherwise lose working from home. I'm a fan of working in coffee shops, too.

Set up regular dates with friends and family. Coffee, lunch, drinks, walks … it doesn't matter as long as you have a general repeating schedule that can become part of your routine. If you and a friend share an interest in an activity, that's even better. See the next section, "Prepare Your Friends and Family" for more.

Start now to take baby steps into interests and hobbies. Get a first tennis lesson on the calendar, pick up some initial supplies for a home garden, learn more about volunteering … Whatever step you take, avoid overwrought research on your computer. Get out of the house and be with other people.

Learn from other professionals whose personality and business overlap. Performers, artists, musicians, public speakers, and yes, other consultants, all have traveled these waters before you. I make it a habit of asking other Independents how they manage their lives. I'm always learning more and have a healthier outlook as a result.

MIND AND BODY.

In addition to mental prep, take steps now to prepare yourself physically. Working independently tends to result in a loss of all those organic breaks that occur in an office, like walking to a colleague's desk, a meeting room across the building, to the bathroom, etc. Plus the ever-presence of your laptop and phone make it harder to stop work for even a little while.

My wife needed over ten years to sell me on this point, but she's right: in addition to its being the right thing, physical exercise helps you to diminish mental stress and increase mentally acuity on the job.

For all of these reasons, preparing yourself should absolutely include you putting good exercise habits in place. And during actual work sessions at home, force yourself to stop and move around. You'll reduce stress, work better, and be able to enjoy the Independent lifestyle for many additional years!

PART 2: PREPARE YOUR FAMILY AND FRIENDS

Yes, you will be the *entire organization*, and yes, you will have a lot more of *you* in your life, but remember that you are not an island in this endeavor. There will always be …

Other people. The next level of your Prep Plan focuses on those people who are closest to you: family, friends, and (perhaps) a trusted colleague or two. If you were to overlook this step, your friends and family could become unwilling sources of friction in your Transition to Independence. But when you prepare this step well, you will create an atmosphere where they are invested in your success and are actively supporting you on your way to greatness!

I emphasize that you absolutely need to have your inner circle aligned with you on the goal of transitioning to Independence. And then, once there, the unique nature of being independent will require ongoing conversations to keep things harmonious with those around you. While I could never tell you how to best manage your closest personal relationships, I can provide summary points on what should be important to you in these conversations and what will likely be important to those closest to you.

THE CONVERSATION TEMPLATE

Talk about what matters. I have had many conversations like these over the years, in good times and in bad. The first thing I've learned is that this kind of conversation requires special treatment. Although you are talking with your spouse or close friends, a topic like this requires a purpose-driven business conversation with a desired outcome. In other words, don't treat this like a conversation about what you're going to watch on Netflix tonight!

Drive the conversation to the right place. I have also learned (mainly through trial and error) that a little bit of planning goes a long way when trying to build alignment. Before you start, be sure that *you* understand the desired outcome of the conversation. Are you looking for buy-in? Advice? To set expectations on time or money? Or, maybe, just to think out loud? Be sure you're clear on what you want—or the problem you're trying to solve—before you start the conversation.

Be patient and listen. Listen well for advice and feedback that you should heed and also the needs and concerns that others share with you. If your conversation is about the actual Transition to Independence, this is an especially important point for your immediate family because they will be taking on the risks and rewards of Independence with you.

Talking About Transition To Independence

A conversation about the transition is a big one. It's many conversations, really, and it will be well served if you give those around you a healthy voice in the dialog. As long as you keep to the goals of the conversation, you and those around you will benefit from taking whatever extra time is needed to work with each other's feedback as you build toward a shared goal for independence.

T2I will have the most impact on your immediate family, so let's focus on conversations with them.

Know what you're talking about. The first, and most important, goal for a discussion with your partner is to help him or her understand what Independence is, why you want to make the change, and how you plan to go about it. Many of the documents that you created in your DiCE Plan should be helpful here. Use them to help illustrate what your work would be like as an independent consultant. In addition, you will certainly be talking about concerns regarding finances, timelines, and the risks associated with Independence, but I encourage you to go further than that.

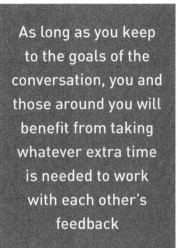

As long as you keep to the goals of the conversation, you and those around you will benefit from taking whatever extra time is needed to work with each other's feedback

Provide a map to the road ahead. The T2I Plan is intended to be a lower-risk method for improving your work-life balance so that *both* of you can enjoy life more. So from the outset, paint a picture of Independence for your partner. Be specific about advancing lifestyle changes along with your career changes. This will keep focus on what you're *really* trying to achieve—and getting your partner aligned on that goal is an exceptionally important step in achieving Independence.

The changes can be big and small. As an example, what might change in the family dynamic if you're not commuting to the office every day? I take the kids to school on certain days to help open up time for my wife's daily schedule. It's a small thing (that works only when I'm not traveling), but it nonetheless improves her day and the overall family dynamic for the two of us and our children.

There is no shortage of examples that can win here: spending more time with your own parents, helping your spouse with his or her career, taking on a long-neglected hobby … Calling these examples by name will help you to incorporate them into the vision for Independence that you and your spouse build and work toward—together.

THE POST-INDEPENDENCE CHAT.

Here's some vital advice that I've come to understand with the help of my wife as we've been "Independent together" over the years: the transition conversation never ends! There is no one-and-done on this topic. When compared to a traditional corporate job, the inherent fluidity of independent work requires a more regular conversation about work and its impacts on lifestyle and family. There will be busts and booms in income, new opportunities that require travel, and times that are steady and at home. And your ability to participate in the family while working from home—the "I'm here, but not here" factor—can vary from day to day.

Managing these dynamics requires active and open communication with your partner and family. Unfortunately, many newly minted Independents don't realize (or were never told of) the need for this heightened level of communication. The unfortunate result is much more stress and frustration at home than necessary—the exact opposite of what Independence is supposed to bring into your life.

So take it from my wife and me: good communication at home is an essential component in achieving and maintaining Independence!

PART 3: PREPARE YOUR ORGANIZATION

We've now talked about preparing yourself and those closest to you for Independence. Now let's expand our view to include the responsibilities and services that you will need to function as a business entity. The good news here is that the list can be quite short for the modern Independent. At no other point in history has an individual person been enabled to do so much with so little. Laptops, the Internet, mobile phones, the rental economy, and (soon) 3D printing are all convening to enable an individual to operate

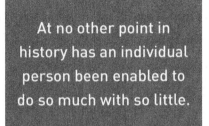

At no other point in history has an individual person been enabled to do so much with so little.

with the weight of an entire team. I call this convergence of ability "Team of One," and it's very exciting for those of us who choose to pursue Independence.

Stick with what you know. Being a Team of One can be a double-edged sword, however, because many Independents get sucked into investing too much of their time in activities that are not related to their expertise or that are otherwise undesirable. This happens to entrepreneurs too: a common example is that a big chunk of your time is spent on sales (like we discussed in the "Prepare Yourself" section), even if it is not your strong suit.

Stick with what you like. It's also okay to admit that you simply don't *want* to take on certain activities like, say, bookkeeping (which has never been on my personal top-ten list). This is especially true if you're being true to the spirit of T2I. What's needed is a strategy that helps you to get started with the least financial risk (a.k.a. Team of One) while also making plans to liberate you from business tasks that don't suit your abilities or desires.

Preparing your organization will help you to do just that by clarifying the full set of tasks that are needed to run your business and make decisions about how and when to allocate those tasks to others. The result is a thoughtful time/money balance for new Independents that can evolve with you to alleviate stress and create more time for focusing on your expertise and your lifestyle in general.

THE GERBER METHOD

Michael E. Gerber describes the best method that I've found for this exercise in his wonderful book, *The E-Myth Revisited*. It's a simple five-step plan that begins by drawing a typical organization chart—the kind with "CEO" or "president" at the top—on a blank piece of paper and then continues with these broad steps:

1. Draw boxes for the standard primary responsibilities that all businesses require: finance, human resources, operations, sales, public relations, etc.

2. Then draw boxes for responsibilities that are specific to your particular expertise and, perhaps, specific business vertical. This may include engineers or developers, for example. And, don't forget to include lead consultant (that's you).

3. Write your initials in the boxes that you know will be your responsibilities for the time being. Items with your initials should include those tasks that you should or want to perform, along with those for which you just don't have a better alternative. Again, sales and bookkeeping are common ones for many Independents.

4. For those boxes that remain blank, add either a "TBD" or fill them in with others' initials if you have a definite resource (perhaps an existing accountant, for example).

5. Go through the chart a final time and highlight the responsibilities in which you genuinely excel and/or love (don't forget to include the CEO role!).

If you're doing this exercise right, you'll find that about three-quarters of the boxes (or more) are assigned to you (see a sample at www.t2iplan.com). While sobering, this is a realistic and okay outcome. Many new Independents get knocked sideways by the unexpected workload that comes with Team of One, but this chart helps to set expectations for you up front. Simply remember that the roles that you have highlighted are the ones that you, personally, will want to keep. Everything else represents a role that you will eventually delegate out to someone else when you have the revenue and success to enable it.

Small Business Services

While still reviewing your chart, you'll see a smaller set of responsibilities that, no matter what, you could never fill. I put most of those responsibilities into the category of *small business services*, and you want to be sure that you have your bases covered here.

Legal: I recommend that you eventually invest the small amount of money needed to form a proper business entity like an LLC (limited liability company). The benefits include: (1) tax benefits (including write offs), (2) liability protection from your personal assets, and (3) a more professional appearance. I used an online service (like legalzoom.com) when I got started. This can save you a couple of thousand dollars, but you'll get less specific advice than you would from a proper lawyer. Weigh your pros and cons appropriately.

Financial: If you do form a business entity, you'll need a bank account to go with it! Here are some tips:

- **Think small.** I have found that most small community banks have lower minimum balances and fewer fees.
- **Look for perks.** A business credit card makes it very easy to track write-offs for tax purposes. The additional points I collect go toward off-season vacations or to visits home to my mom and dad.
- **Keep track.** Get in the habit now of using a personal online finance-tracking service like Mint. It helps with personal budgeting and further facilitates tracking of business expenses.

- **Find a money man.** I recommend you review your entire T2I Plan with your accountant. If you don't have one, you might find that it's worth a certain amount of money to get a review.

Healthcare: While not a responsibility, per se, healthcare is often the primary benefit of a corporate job. If your spouse or partner has this benefit, the best path is to go with that. Others options exist, of course, and most states now have a healthcare exchange for individuals seeking coverage. Take time to account for this in advance and include it in conversations with your family.

Public relations and marketing: These services are especially important for a new Independent. We will take a closer look in the next section.

I take myself through the organization plan about once a year so that I can keep pace with the evolving demands of my own business environment. I might assign someone new to an existing box or add or remove a box or two. In some years, I find that no changes are necessary, and I simply validate that I'm in a 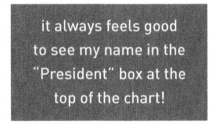 good place. No matter what, it always feels good to see my name in the "President" box at the top of the chart!

PART 4: PREPARE YOUR BRAND

I should state for the record that I know more than a few successful consultants who have *no* brand whatsoever; they do quite well with nothing more than a generic email address, a solid reputation, and a good contact list. Not all of us are so gifted, however. For most Independents, a bit of branding presents a more professional appearance that can help to close business and set higher rates. The list of necessary materials is relatively short: a logo, a website, business cards, a presentation template, social-media accounts (including LinkedIn), and perhaps a blog.

> For most Independents, a bit of branding presents a more professional appearance that can help to close business and set higher rates.

If you'd like to take your brand further, such as with a mission statement or a commitment to a specific cause, I'm all for it. My experiences and observations have taught me, however, to start with *good enough* in this area and invest more time and money as your success justifies it. Either way, when you complete this "Prepare Your Brand" step, the result should be a set of these materials that are good enough to use immediately in sales efforts, which we cover in detail in chapter 5.

Here are the three steps we're about to go through next.

1. Fine-tune your DiCE Plan
2. Select your name and logo
3. Update and create your new branded materials

Fine-Tune Your DiCE Plan

In step 5 ("Foundational Marketing Materials") of your DiCE Plan (page 37), we used the creation of those documents as a vehicle to help you define, for yourself, what your specific consulting expertise will be. Since then, you've had more time to think about your transition and—very importantly—have discussed it in detail with your close family and friends.

Ask yourself: Have those conversations helped you to evolve what you stated in your title, job description, or value-add statement? If *yes*, you should refine your work now, before committing more resources to preparing your brand any further. Along the same lines, I recommend that you take another pass at googling your title and job description so that you can reconfirm that you're using terms that others are looking for.

Select Your Name and Logo

You've defined a title and a job description, but how about a *company* name? While certainly not necessary, a good name might help to further describe your work and/or lend a level of credibility. I have colleagues that go with their initials, their name, a play on their specialty, or perhaps a geographical region. All of the above are just fine, as long as your choice isn't too long, isn't too clever, and is easy enough to pronounce. Example: I started as "The Zwas Group" and then evolved to "Zwas Group" a few years later because a friend suggested that it was hard to pronounce *the* and *Zwas* in quick succession.

Regarding logos, a nice logo *feels* good and can lend an aura of a more experienced professionalism. But, I have always been happy with my good-enough approach to this. When I started, a friend (another Independent) gave me a deal on some logo-design work as she did my first website. Many years later, I stepped it up a notch, but only because I knew that "this consulting thing" was going to stick and that my success to that point justified a little more investment. If you aren't fortunate enough to have any graphic-artist friends, there are a handful of options that will help you to get a good logo that are within the range of a justified investment. Consider the online 99designs, along with professionals from usual services like Upwork and Craigslist.

Update and Create Your New Branded Materials

This step combines your fine-tuned statements, your name, and your logo into the materials that represent your brand—i.e., you! These details are more important than you might think. It's about appearances, and this is an area in which an intelligent approach to appearances can become a handsome reality. Let's take a closer look ...

Your Website:

In my experience, the most common scenario for an independent consultant's website is for it to be viewed by people who you've already met in person or who have been referred to you by a colleague or friend. In this case, your site serves to augment those impressions and to put your best foot forward.

Starting with the draft website you created as part of your DiCE plan, make updates so that it remains consistent with your evolved title, job description, and value-add statement. If you feel the need to make additional cosmetic changes, make them at this time, too. Remember to start with good-enough, and then when you 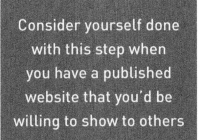 are ready, buy a proper domain name (via GoDaddy, for example) that is based on your company name.

Consider yourself done with this step when you have a published website that you'd be willing to show to others. We're not going to advertise its existence quite yet, but it is important to have it there.

Your Email Address:

Just like your website, a proper email presence signifies to clients that you are an experienced professional. As an example, *aaron@zwasgroup.com* will always be better than the generic *aaronzwas3@yahoo.com*. Take the time to set up your branded email address (via your website host or Gmail, for example), and remember to create a signature with the same details that you'd use on a business card. If you designed a logo, include that too.

Your LinkedIn Profile:

Unlike some social networks, LinkedIn is mandatory for Independents. A link to a relevant article and a simple comment now and then is perfect: your content is presented to potential readers in the right forum, is easily shared, and is not too much overhead for you. In this step, update your LinkedIn profile like your website: based on your fine-tuned DiCE plan. Don't publish the updated version yet, but have it in hand for when you're ready to fully transition.

Blogs and other Social Content:

A blog is a great way to demonstrate expertise. The downside is that you have to keep it up! A blog with three entries from last year is hardly going to send the right message to prospective clients. So if you choose to take this on, know that it is a real responsibility and should be accounted for in your org chart from the "Prepare Your Organization" section in this chapter.

> A blog is a great way to demonstrate expertise. The downside is that you have to keep it up!

After LinkedIn, Twitter is currently my second choice for Independents' business content and news. If you choose to do so, now is the time to set up that account. Remember that it's generally best to set up social accounts that are distinct from any personal ones you might have already.

Business Cards:

I rarely use business cards these days, but you're not complete without them. My take here is that less is more. Include your name and title, your company name, one email address, and one phone number. Your mailing address is not necessary, and please, don't include a fax number.

Other Materials:

When I got started, I took some extra time to create templates for client-facing documents like proposals, invoices, and just a standard presentation (PowerPoint) template. Doing so up front cleared my head for the actual content of those proposals when the opportunities presented themselves. Use whatever applications you prefer (Microsoft Word and PowerPoint work for me), and remember *good enough*: include your logo and then color-coordinate the rest of your templates around that. If you'd like a more thorough list of templates you are likely to need, see t2iplan.com for more.

PART 5: PREPARE YOUR WORKSPACE

When I tell people what I do for a living, the working-from-home part always gets the most attention. People either love the idea or say something like "I could never do that. I would be too distracted." Either way, there's always a reaction, and the topic is an increasingly hot one. In the past fifteen years, I have seen the old taboos of working from home melt away as I encounter more and more people who are working from home one day a week or re-entering the workforce in a remote capacity.

As an Independent, however, you will not really have a choice! From kitchen tables to rented start-up space, you will likely work in a variety of non-traditional settings. And depending on your personality and home environment, it *is* easy to get distracted or frustrated. It is also easy for your cohabitants (usually, your family) to get frustrated too. Everyone has to share the same space; there are errands to run, home projects to complete, and the plain-old temptations of a gorgeous day that is begging for a bike ride, a run, or perhaps catching up on the latest TV series that everyone is talking about.

This at-home dynamic is a key component of Independence. How do you strike the right balance between being effective while working and enjoying all of the benefits that working from home should offer? There's no set way, but I can assure you, a way will be found—even if from necessity.

> How do you strike the right balance between being effective while working and enjoying all of the benefits that working from home should offer?

Lucky for you, I know a lot about this topic. I've been working from home, in varying degrees, since 1999. In that time, my home situation has gone from single (with roommates and without), to cohabitating (in boyfriend and husband capacities), to three babies being born (the oldest now in third grade). I've worked and lived in the small second-floor of a row house in Brooklyn, cramped apartments in Manhattan, urban townhouses, and now an actual house with a front yard and a dedicated room for an office. In all of these scenarios, my hours-per-week in the home office have ranged from ten to eighty hours (yes, eighty) per week. And I've also worked from all of those other places I mentioned earlier: coffee shops, hotel lobbies, libraries, friends' couches and kitchen tables, my parents' house during extended visits, and—when I'm fortunate enough to do it—vacation resorts and rentals.

Through it all, I've been increasing my income by an average of 25 percent per year since my arrival in New York in 1999 and figuring out how to live the life of a true Independent.

When I think about the working aspects of Independence, I tend to think about this in three categories:

1. Working from home as a lifestyle (a.k.a. how to *be* in the home office)
2. The fundamentals of a good home office
3. Tips for working out of the house

How to BE in Your Home Office

I cannot tell you how often people have told me that "I don't know if I could work from home. I'd never get anything done!" Don't buy it. It's likely that you will work *more,* not less, at home than you do in any office. My advice here falls into five guidelines that will help you to be productive while also creating every opportunity to take advantage of Independence.

Create a Routine

People who work in an office have to *go to work* each day. That's the routine. Working from home should be no different. Even when you are at home, work is work, and you need a routine to support it. I won't lecture you on brushing your teeth in the morning, but all of the obvious basics still apply: wake up at a proper time, get ready for the day, have breakfast, etc.

The good news is that, while you still need a routine, you can have a *new* routine. Your *new* routine should have built-in details that take advantage of an Independent lifestyle. It's a great opportunity: you now have time to work out in the morning because you no longer have to commute. You can take the kids to school. You can take 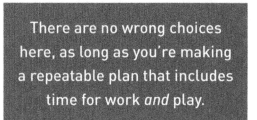 thirty minutes just to enjoy coffee and a magazine before starting your day. There are no wrong choices here, as long as you're making a repeatable plan that includes time for work *and* play.

There are no wrong choices here, as long as you're making a repeatable plan that includes time for work *and* play.

I've learned a lot about home-office routines during my pajama-clad tenure. Here are some of the highlights.

First timers: It takes time to ease into it. Don't fret too much if you're working on home projects in the middle of the day for the first couple of weeks. Just be mindful of what you are doing and get better as time goes by.

Don't let your routine become dogma. Break patterns to have lunch with friends or to enjoy other special events. And if you're fighting a stretch of unproductiveness, stop. Go take care of the shopping list that's in the back of your head instead. Whatever your reason, just know that you'll have to return to the desk later when you're more focused and ready to work, even if that's in the evening.

Do today's work today. This is a big one: resist the urge to push today's work till tomorrow. Procrastination will steal all your freedom if you don't keep it under arrest. If you're out during the day, get the work done at night.

> Procrastination will steal all your freedom if you don't keep it under arrest.

No TV. TV shows (even if watched on your computer) are for the evening, as a reward for a full day of work. Unless it is somehow integral to your line of work (like market news on Bloomberg, for example), do not interact with the TV during normal working hours. I mean it!

Set Boundaries

Laptop computers, broadband Internet at home, and mobile phones have enabled the expectation that we should be responding to email in every waking moment! And this challenge is even more acute in a home-office environment because everything—your desk, notes, and paperwork—is right under your nose. It's much harder to escape, both mentally and physically. Combine this with the knowledge that Independents have thin safety nets, and you have a situation that is almost guaranteed to drive you to work every waking minute of the day.

The solution to this challenge is to define good boundaries. Life/work boundaries help you to be in the moment —to be present and truly enjoy the important aspects of Independence. Boundaries set expectations with your family and friends, too. Should they wait to have dinner with you? Do they know that you'll be available for coffee or school drop-off in the morning? Simple rules keep you healthy, productive, and in a good place with those around you.

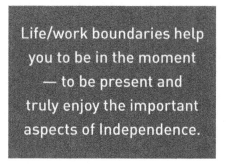

Life/work boundaries help you to be in the moment — to be present and truly enjoy the important aspects of Independence.

For those of you with a strong work ethic, this section applies to you, too! Even if you work long hours, put boundaries in place that force you to stop now and then. If you don't heed my advice, I guarantee that you will (1) turn yourself into a prisoner in your own home office, missing out on the whole point of Independence, and (2) burn out.

Full disclosure on this particular topic: my wife will quickly confirm that I'm not the best at practicing what I preach here. I have collaborated for years with a core group of people who are tough successful professionals: the consulting equivalent of the Marines, if you will, and we work long hours. But, I usually have breakfast and dinner each weekday with the family. Then, if I need to, I pick up work again in the evening after the kids are in bed.

> **Border patrol.** Here are some examples of boundaries that I try to keep and that you might want to consider:
> - No work earlier than seven o'clock a.m. or later than seven o'clock p.m.
> - No work on weekends, unless it's one to two hours early in the morning
> - Not working means not working. Specifically, not checking or responding to email
>
> Be selective in your exceptions (because they will occur) and communicate them early to those closest to you.

Take Mental Breaks

Whereas setting boundaries focuses on the macro scale between work and life, this point is on the micro-scale: in order to maintain productivity during your working hours, you must take regular breaks. Independents have to make a conscious effort to meet this need because the standard organic distractions of an office do not usually exist at home. There is no water cooler. You will not bump into colleagues on the way to the bathroom, break room, or parking lot. There is no one sitting next to you or down the hall for a quick conversation or asking you out for lunch. In appropriate measure these distractions are beneficial: they get you up and moving, thinking about something else for a moment, and generally give your brain a chance to pause and recalibrate.

Home workers have to create their own distractions. Now I know that some of you are thinking, "that won't be a problem!" But, you'll see. Once Independents get over the initial transition of working from home, they run a high risk of being shut-ins who work very long stretches without pause. When you work from home, it is likely that solitude is your enemy. So stop yourself now and then. Chances are you'll still be working in the back of your head as you prepare lunch, take a walk, or even read the news (or Facebook) for ten minutes.

It's even okay to *putter*. I used to think that I was wasting time as I organized my closet or raked leaves in the backyard in the middle of the day. No longer: as long as a client isn't waiting for anything, I've learned that I'm actually much more productive when I take time out for a small extra-curricular activity here and there.

Of course, all of this is in the context of the rules for routine and boundaries that I describe above. I always am sure to do *today's* work *today*. I'm simply showing you here how to work within those rules without making yourself a slave to your laptop. So buy stuff on Amazon, run to the store, organize your kitchen drawers—it's all okay in moderation!

THE ART OF THE BREAK

Learn to move. As far as Independence goes, I do a good job in creating short mental breaks in the form of DIY projects, home repairs, and being with the kids. My wife (who is a choreographer and has a vested interest in fitness) can attest to the fact that I'm less-good with physical breaks. It's not that I don't believe in fitness; it's just that spontaneous physical exercise doesn't come naturally to me. Come to think of it, neither does planned physical exercise. Hmmm.

But my wife is right: leaving the desk for a walk, a run, a stretch, some yoga, or a quick workout are all good things. Choose one. The research here is conclusive: you are more likely to encounter myriad health challenges (including, notably, a shorter lifespan) by parking yourself in a desk chair for hours at a time every day. If you're doing it right, your routine will have physical activity built right in, and your short breaks will be mental/physical combos. As time goes by, I get a little better at this—even if I'm doing a few quick exercises right at my desk. Although I'm not quick to take on physical activity, I never regret it after the fact. I'm always more productive and feel good knowing that I'm doing the right thing.

Don't set guidelines on your own and in secret

As a final guideline, be sure that you develop your version of work-from-home in collaboration with those closest to you. This an extension of the "Prepare Your Family and Friends" conversations we discussed above.

> ...be sure that you develop your version of work-from-home in collaboration with those closest to you.

Once your routines are established, remember that it is equally important to communicate openly when you know that they will change. When I see a lot of work coming my way, for example, I do my best to give my wife as much advance warning as possible. This allows her and the family to adjust for a few days. When work gets under control again, we switch back to giving my wife more time in the mornings and evenings, and I reemerge back into polite society.

With good ongoing communication, I (really, my wife and I) have made my office work in a Manhattan apartment with a newborn. And we've done it in a townhouse with three children under the age of five. And even my kids know the score: they learned early that they can't talk to Dad when he's on the phone. Does that work all the time? No. Is it better than being in an office and not seeing them until six o'clock p.m. each day? Sure is!

The fundamentals of a good home office

A good home office does not necessarily require a dedicated room. In fact, I've learned over the years that it is the small things that have the greatest impact on fostering a positive working environment. Later, if your success justifies it, you can spend time and money on expensive furniture and other equipment. For your transition, however, check your preparedness against this simple list. It covers all the bases for enabling your success while limiting additional home-office expenses. If you would like more detail than what I share here, you can see www. t2iplan.com for more on home office setup, equipment, and services.

YOUR HOME OFFICE CHECKLIST

Put a tick next to each of these once you've thought it through enough to have a strategy:

Mobile phone plan: It's about to go way up! Don't get caught by surprise and wind up paying fees.

Headset: Working remotely means lots of time on the phone, and often in public spaces (which might include your kitchen if you have a young and hungry family). You want to be sure that your clients can hear you absolutely clearly, that you sound composed and professional, and that you aren't getting headaches and neck cramps after five-hour phone sessions. Spend a couple of extra dollars, if you can, on a comfortable headset with a noise-cancelling microphone.

Home Internet: In the modern era, no Internet = no business. So if you haven't already, consider paying a few extra dollars a month for increased speeds to help support screen shares, video chats, and overall dependability. Your Wi-Fi router should fall into this category, too. If you have the opportunity to upgrade to a stronger signal for a hundred dollars or less, it's probably worth the investment.

Backup: As an Independent, you have no IT team to help bail you out in the event of a lost laptop or similar. So don't skip this detail, please. Use Dropbox, Google Drive, or any other cloud-storage service to back up your documents. Add further support with a hard backup on a USB drive.

Go-to spaces for specific tasks: Don't get caught out trying to find the right place to take an important call: do some up-front reconnaissance of local coffee houses, libraries, diners, etc. And make a home plan, too. In addition to my proper office, I have go-to spaces for quiet phone calls, deep thinking, and options for "just doing email."

Notice anything missing from this list? Perhaps items like *office* or *desk*? This is intentional. I want you to understand how little you really need to make your home office a reality. From my point of view, everything beyond this is a nice-to-have that should be developed in tandem with your established success.

Tips for Working Out of the House

While I always recommend the establishment of a viable home-office environment, one of the best parts of Independence is that you can work nearly anywhere that has mobile and internet access. Below are a few considerations on how to make the most of this fun and cost-effective opportunity.

SIX WAYS TO SPOT A GOOD DEAL IN OFFICE SPACE

If you think that a shared workspace might be right for you, I encourage you to try out a few. Don't be taken in by the first one you see. Instead, look for the following positive characteristics:

1. **Pay as you go:** You should be allowed to either pay per-visit or a small monthly fee for unlimited (i.e. daily) use.
2. **Community:** Look for something that *feels good*—the experience, including the people, are part of what you're paying for! You want a combination of good energy plus colleagues that offer services you might need and who might also be possible referral sources. The best workspaces actively foster a community with after-hours social and networking events.
3. **Good physical space:** Again, you want something that feels good. Big, bright, open. A good variety of tables, couches, and other workspaces. Dedicated conference rooms for clients or special work sessions are a nice extra touch.
4. **Utilities:** Internet should be included in the price.
5. **Local:** Don't replace your long commute to work with a long commute to the workspace! Find something nearby.
6. **Good coffee:** Good coffee = good productivity. Go ahead and judge your workspace by the quality of their coffee!

Rented Space:

I've dabbled with rented and shared office space for years. For nearly all Independents, the better choice is a *shared space*—which will have a lower price point and more dynamic office experience—versus a dedicated rented office suite that has its own lock and key.

Working in public:

I go through phases where I work a lot in public and then shift back home. It usually boils down to phone calls: more calls means more time in my home office, where it is easier to control background noise.

But if I have a long stretch of quiet time (or time when I do my *real* work, as I like to say), I'll opt for a public place that has the best combination of quality coffee, solid Internet, and not too much noise. It's a great way to fight the isolation of working from home. I buy something every few hours, get to know the staff, and tip generously.

The lobbies of mid-range and high-end hotels can be great places to work, too. They usually have free Internet and a good mix of people coming through.

Regardless of the location, I always bring my noise-cancelling headset (for the inevitable phone call that will still find me), and I try to make the most of the situation by stacking up a social or casual business meeting in the same (or nearby) venue.

Routine on the Road:

Working from on-the-road places like the homes of friends and family and vacation destinations is obviously one of the highlights of Independence, and I've personally had a pretty good run in this area. It turns out that my personal best use of this flexibility has been in the margins; I've extended many weekend trips by two or three days over the years. Being able to work in that manner without paperwork, formal approval, and HR professionals has been truly liberating.

"Roll" models: I work with others who have taken their "remote offices" down the street, out of town, and to a whole other level. Consider:

- Tamara, who changes her city, or at least her neighborhood, each month. She rents apartments through Airbnb and takes with her no more than she can carry from her car up to a second floor walkup.
- Scot, who lives and works out of a flatbed camper, drives across the American West to rock climbing and ski sites, which he explores on off hours. He recently kept standard office hours while living and camping in Guatemala for six weeks, including eight days in a tent on the side of a dormant volcano!

What you might find surprising is that the approach used by Tamara and Scot for successful on-the-road work is the same that you should use in more common examples like, say, adding an extra day to Memorial Day Weekend. The key is to either (a) work, or (b) don't work. It sounds trite, but most of us are 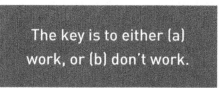 likely to fall into semi-work situations that are in limbo. Such situations take more time, result in work of lesser quality, and—most importantly—diminish the very experience that you're supposed to be enjoying!

If you choose to work on the road, establish a light routine and communicate it to those around you. For me, that usually means shutting myself in a room (or a coffee shop; yes, there is a pattern) for a few hours, setting one to three simple goals, and getting them done. Then I get back to the main event—the beach, the family event, whatever—with a clear mind and no lingering thoughts about work.

One final note about working on the road: I do not usually disclose to my clients that I'll be in another location unless (1) the time zones are notably different, (2) Internet access might be limited, or (3) I'm really taking time off (like for a family wedding). As long as expectations are set in advance and the work is getting done, I've never had an issue with this approach.

PREP PLAN RECAP

If you've made it this far in the book, congratulations! To review, here's what you've accomplished by completing your Prep Plan

1. **Yourself:** You have set expectations for yourself and begun to prepare mentally, physically, and financially.

2. **Your Family, Friends, and Colleagues:** You have set expectations with them, gained buy-in, and defined what your shared version of Independence will look like.

3. **Your Organization:** You have created a responsibilities plan and a short list of required services for Independents.

4. **Your Brand:** You have fine-tuned your brand's look and feel and applied it to appropriate official materials.

5. **Your Workspace (Wherever It May Be):** You have set best practices for working at home, in public, and on the road.

Add all that together with completing your Define Your Consulting Expertise (DiCE) plan from chapter 3, and you've accomplished quite a lot, indeed.

Giant steps. Not only have you achieved at least two big steps in the T2I Plan, you've done so while being smart about:
- committing your precious resources, time, and money carefully
- baking in considerations for an optimal Independent experience *and* a best-possible lifestyle for you and your family
- focusing on getting your close family and friends on board for supporting you in this exciting new chapter in your life

To me, that all sounds like a big deal. Wouldn't you agree?

So high-fives all around! Have a modest celebration; you've come much farther than most. I'm positive that you could start taking your first gigs tomorrow, if necessary. So how *do* you pick up those important first gigs? And what about that minor detail of your current employer? Move on to the next chapter to learn more about how to ramp up your initial independent work while elegantly leaving your current employer. And, as always, see the t2iplan.com website for additional help.

CHAPTER 5

Step 3: Transition with Confidence

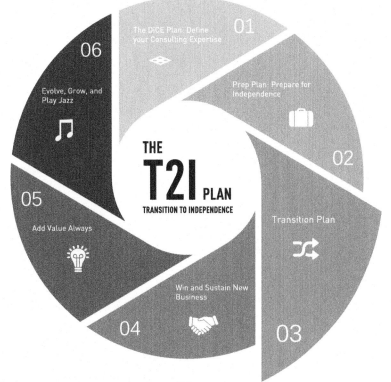

At this point in the T2I Plan, your value-add is straightforward and clear, your materials are ready, your friends and family understand what's happening next, and you have an appropriate home office for your independent work.

Now let's get you some actual business.

In this chapter we will talk specifically about your first forays into independent consulting. This phase is particularly crucial because it captures the actual moments of transition from your current job to independence.  There are real risks as you transition from that dependability to the less predictable state of an Independent. The plan itself requires finesse and real decision-making on your part. Also, in this chapter, I define small safe steps that will diminish the unknown while still moving you forward—but you will have to continually assess your current state and tolerance for risk as you proceed.

As in the prior chapters, I'll lay out our plan here and then dive into the details in order. Here's what we are about to cover ...

- Part 1: Prime the Pump
- Part 2: Moonlighting and Part-Time Work
- Part 3: When to Leave and How to Do It

Warning: the sections of this chapter won't necessarily occur in a linear fashion for you. In fact, it's likely that your overall transition will ebb and flow for quite some time. With that in mind, this chapter will give you enough information so that you will understand your position amongst the waves, so to speak, and help you to keep your eye out for land. Maintaining this longer view serves as your North Star; it helps to maintain your resolve and to inform your short-term decisions in a way that will minimize your risk *and* serve the big picture.

PART 1: PRIME THE PUMP

As we mentioned in the "Prepare Yourself" section of the previous chapter, you are about to become your own vice president of sales, whether you like it or not. And for many Independents, gaining *escape velocity* (i.e., getting enough initial business) is the make-or-break factor. Most of us understand that we need to *be in rotation* and *get the word*

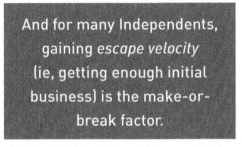

And for many Independents, gaining *escape velocity* (ie, getting enough initial business) is the make-or-break factor.

out. Plus, we have a vague sense that *networking* will somehow produce the desired effects. But what are the specific activities? And how, exactly, do they translate to an actual check in the mail? Great resources are available to help you take your expertise in this area to the highest level. I will lay out the fundamentals here and give you enough to get started on the right path.

Before we get into the tactics, let's talk objectives. Defining what you are trying to achieve will help you to play to your personal strengths and the needs of your specific situation. In order of decreasing priority, my objectives for networking are ...

- obtaining new clients
- building relationships with potential referrers
- gathering information that helps in becoming a more informed specialist
- evolving the pitch (through practice and observing others)
- finding kindred spirits with whom to trade stories and advice, about both work and the Independent lifestyle

Got it?

All of the prep work that you've done so far will support these objectives. Your value-add statement, business cards, and new website (among other things) will support a clear and credible message that resonates with clients and that can be accurately shared by referring friends and colleagues. As long as you're meeting one or two of the above objectives, you're doing a great job. Keeping the objectives in mind, let's have a look at the primary set of activities that will help you attract your first gigs, starting with that website of yours and including the digital resources available to you.

Tactic: Start Producing Ongoing Content

When we discussed building your branded materials on page 62, we focused on static content. That is, content that you write and then let sit for long stretches of time—your *about* page, your name, contact information, etc. In order to really prime the pump, however, you have to activate your ongoing digital content—the stuff that appears in LinkedIn activity (like shares and comments), blogs, Twitter accounts, and possibly a video channel such as YouTube.

Caution: Time suck ahead. If you're not careful, content creation can suck up a lot of time. So you want a lightweight approach to ongoing content that gets you the most bang for your buck. Your work should therefore be specific to your consulting expertise and created in a style that helps you to get things published in a timely manner without agonizing over perfection.

I've developed my approach to content by learning from others; it helps me to achieve the following primary benefits in the most efficient way possible:
1. You demonstrate your expertise and professional point of view (aka *value*) through a body of work that grows over time.
2. You become more knowledgeable as you continually reference current events and trends related to work.

For me, source material comes from two primary sources: reading and personal experience.

Create Ongoing Content from What You Read ...

Reading for profit. As it turns out, more than half of your *content* time should be focused on reading, not writing. If you're not doing so already, now is a great time to get into the habit of professional reading. Give yourself thirty minutes a day to read what others have to say from within your profession.

Dragging a net. To help you find relevant content, consider setting up simple Google Alerts (or similar) based on keywords like profession, potential clients, and big players in your industry. You'll get an email summary each day that guides you to content that's worth reading. You will also find good material from others' LinkedIn posts and social channels, along with industry journals and websites.

Passing it on. Once you have a stream of appropriate incoming content, contribute to the dialog by sharing, liking, and linking to the good stuff. When you do share, add a quick sentence or two of your own. This is very much in the spirit of the web, of course, and is a win-win for the original authors (who still get credit, plus additional readership) and you (as you begin to gain a toehold and find your voice in a professional conversation).

Example: Links to others' stories with a quick summary or comment is a perfect contribution. (Note: Although I recommend that you not publish your updated LinkedIn profile yet, there is no harm in starting to share small amounts of relevant content through your current LinkedIn profile.)

Create Ongoing Content from Personal Experience

Your workplace observations and conversations with others are the seeds of great content. Example: A short paragraph that begins with "Over coffee yesterday, a colleague shared a professional problem she's running into at work..." Add your high-level thoughts on how to solve that problem, and just like that, you've demonstrated advisory knowledge—perfect for a short blog or video post.

> Your workplace observations and conversations with others are the seeds of great content.

A wonderful side benefit of ongoing content is that you always have something new to discuss when talking with people in person. Let's keep this in mind as we move to the next section and discuss one-on-one conversations.

Tactic: Develop Individual Connections

Despite the global reach of the Internet, most Independents whom I know develop their business from personal connections. As with content curation, however, we want a time-effective way for developing these connections. My approach below is not exactly rocket science, but it is a time-tested and effective five-step plan for succeeding in broadening your network of connections.

Step 1: Build a list of contacts.

Organize it by: (1) potential clients, (2) potential referrers, and (3) potential advice. Regarding current clients, I encourage you to test the waters regarding opportunities for independent business with current corporate clients and former colleagues. Remember to always use discretion, honor your employment contract, and be honest.

Step 2: Draft a template email.

Do this for each category. To make it easier for you, the templates can be up to 75 percent the same, with minor variations as appropriate.

A well-templated email should have these five important characteristics:
1. **A two-sentence summary** of your new endeavor and value-add
2. **A specific request** for business, referrals, or advice
3. **A personalized element,** where you call the person by name and maybe drop in a line about a personal detail[1]
4. **A specific call to action** to schedule a proper conversation in the next few weeks, like a quick phone call, or coffee
5. **A simple thank-you** is always a good idea

See t2iplan.com for an example.

_____

1. *My advice: If you don't have a strong enough connection for this, they probably don't know you that well either. Drop them from the list.*

Step 3: Meet in person.

Be clear in defining the specific ask in your email and aim for one simple goal like one referral or a bit of feedback.

Use the tools from your DiCE Plan and Prep Plan! Your title, job description, value-add, latest industry news…

Make business personal. Make sure you focus on the person. You're in the relationship business now, so be present to your guests' stories and what you have in common. Be mindful that these meetings are often a favor—don't be too pushy and be sensitive to your guest's time constraints.

Step 4: Follow-up.

Send a short and gracious email within twenty-four hours of your conversation. Summarize your pitch and the *simple goal* you defined. Then give it two weeks and send a pleasant follow-up if you don't hear anything. A second reminder is okay, but then you should drop it—again, graciously.

Step 5: Repeat.

Keep working these simple steps and be consistent. This is how you get the word out with your local sphere of contacts.

> *A note on cold calling:* My personal advice: *don't bother.* A small percentage of people have it in their DNA to do this sort of thing, but it makes the rest of us (myself included) nauseous. Focus on building real relationships, not getting shot down by strangers. (But see page 99 for the one exception.)

Tactic: Attend Events and Join Groups and Associations

Working individual connections gives you the opportunity to convey a nuanced description of your value-add, but your reach will necessarily be limited. Larger groups and events offer the opposite: a broader reach, but with a message that is less deep. While there is certainly value in this type of networking, most events, groups, and associations are for-profit endeavors. Tread carefully here and assess critically the return you might get on any group-level investment.

To put it in perspective, the primary benefits I've realized in this area have been (1) finding a few kindred spirits with whom I can talk shop and trade advice, and (2) practicing my pitch and observing others doing the same.

Professional Associations

Professional Associations are a good idea in general—even outside of physical events. There are hundreds, if not thousands, of such organizations, ranging from local commerce and small business groups to specifics like event planners, music therapists, truck drivers, nurses, and everything in between.

Internet searches and social media will help you to quickly find groups, communities, and forums that can keep you connected with your professional specialty.

The benefits ...
- keeping up with the latest and greatest in your area of expertise
- getting connected with others who might have extra work to pass around
- having fun talking shop, sharing common grievances, and basically swimming in the language of your specialty for a while

Watch out for ...
- specialists who don't know how to sell
- a tight distinction between what is interesting to specialists vs. what the market needs

Industry-Specific Events

Industry-specific events and conventions could be for your profession or for your target set of clients.

The benefits …

- same as professional associations, but on a larger scale
- a room full of potential clients

Watch out for …

- the high cost of these events, especially for Independents (hotel rooms, airfare, etc.)
- possible absence of actual decision-makers

Networking Groups

These groups are a curated collection of individuals who usually meet once a month to share advice and contacts with each other. Some are free. Some are not. Some are structured. Some are loose.

The benefits …

- discussions with motivated people who are not in competition with each other and, hopefully, have complementary professions

Watch out for …

- ineffectiveness. The group has to feel good to be effective. Ask yourself: Is it easy to get to the meetings? Do you like and trust the people? Are they useful to you? Are you useful to them?

General Networking Events

Unlike networking *groups*, these networking *events* are often in the evening and in bars. I include general chamber of commerce and alma mater events in this category.

The benefits …

- many rapid-fire opportunities to practice your pitch
- the opportunity to observe others doing the same and learning from both the good and bad
- "opportunities" that have nothing to do with work (remembering that we're in a bar)

Watch out for …

- events that are occasionally fun but rarely yield new business
- "opportunities" that have nothing to do with work (again, remembering that we're in a bar)

The takeaway: An Independent's need for priming the pump never goes away—even the most successful among us need to foster a steady stream of ongoing business! So be mindful of which tactics work for you best and actively evolve your own best way. It's a skill set that will serve you well for a long time to come.

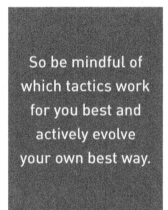

So be mindful of which tactics work for you best and actively evolve your own best way.

The caveat: Include these activities in your time allowance. Budgeting your time will help avoid the pitfalls of overinvolvement.

BEAUTIFUL IN THE MOONLIGHT . . .

The benefits of the moonlighting approach boil down to three big items:

1. **Increased experience.** You are working on your own, which contributes to increased confidence, additional references, and more source material for ongoing content.
2. **Smoother transition.** There is a smaller bridge to cross from when you quit your current job to full financial stability as an Independent.
3. **A failsafe.** You are maintaining the safety net of your current full-time employment.

The trade-offs, of course, are that you will have to work more (often in the evenings) and that this limited additional work will not replace your entire income in one sweep.

PART 2: MOONLIGHTING AND PART-TIME WORK

If your prime-the-pump efforts go well, they will lead to your first independent business opportunities. Remember that my overarching advice through your Transition to Independence is *safety first*. So I recommend that you explore these opportunities as moonlighting gigs—opportunities that you pursue while maintaining your full-time employment.

The Rules of Engagement

This stage can be one of the most stressful and risky in your Transition to Independence. You can minimize these factors by maintaining the right attitude and best possible communications with those closest to you.

Your current employer continues to deserve your best throughout your transition. While I do not recommend that you talk with your employer (yet) about this topic, it is important to maintain the quality and integrity of your work at the office.

Play by the rules. Do not conduct your independent work from your employer's office, on your employer's computers and phones, or during times when you are expected to be on the job. In addition to legal concerns, it is the right thing to do—and remember that former employers can often write great referrals and make great clients!

Your family and friends should be informed and consulted as we defined in your Prep Plan (chapter 4). If you're going to be working in earnest in the evenings, you won't be as available for social activities, family responsibilities, etc. Get ahead of this by continuing to set expectations with those around you. If your life has the structure to support it, try to define set working hours (like from eight o'clock p.m. to ten o'clock p.m. and a few hours on Saturday mornings).

Options and Sources for Moonlighting Gigs

At this point in your transition, the right opportunity matters more than bringing in some cash. You want to avoid the yeah-I-could-do-that stuff and focus on opportunities that are direct matches with your value-add. It is these latter opportunities that will best demonstrate your expertise and help you to fetch higher rates.

...focus on opportunities that are direct matches with your value-add.

Between your personal connections, a broad range of professional organizations, and online marketplaces like Upwork, there are often hundreds of potential opportunities waiting for you. It's an embarrassment of riches out there, and you need to choose wisely.

SMART MOONLIGHTING STRATEGIES

- **Direct referrals and connections** are almost always best. These are gigs achieved directly as a result of your prime-the-pump efforts.
- **Subcontracting** is also a great source of business. A certain percentage of your rate will go to the primary contractor, but you do not have to find the clients, and you're likely to get helpful feedback from the consultant (or similar) who hires you.
- **Website marketplaces** like Upwork are the one-night-stands of independent work: many quick opportunities, but they will generally be shallow—with limited feedback, lower rates, and less potential for repeat business.
- **Teaching** night classes at smaller local colleges is a less-common but reasonable opportunity for moonlighters. The revenue isn't enormous, but it lends credibility to your expertise and can be fun and rewarding in its own right. Plus, teaching a course (or even preparing for a seminar) further forces you to organize your pitch and best practices—something that is always useful.
- **Volunteering** is a similar opportunity. Find an organization that fits into your category and make yourself useful to the organization—and vice-versa of course.

SHORT ANSWERS TO KEY QUESTIONS

Regardless of how a moonlighting opportunity presents itself to you, consider the following:

1. Will you be able to build a solid, demonstrable experience from the work?
2. Is the client likely to provide repeat or ongoing business?
3. Does the client seem likely to provide referrals?
4. Does the client seem likely to provide meaningful feedback that will help you to improve?
5. How much time will it take to create a proposal?
6. About how long will it take for the client to make a decision?
7. Will you be able to charge a sustainable rate for your work?

Six of these need only simple yes/no responses, and one can be answered with a number. If you don't have seven answers, take the time to think them through.

Build Your Moonlighting Work into Something Bigger

Remember, as you work on a project that the value is for your *client.* When you complete that effort, however, you have to find the value that work can provide to *you.* Especially when in the middle of the T2I Plan, it is important to ensure that each ounce of your work can be built into the bigger picture. This is one of the secrets of successful consultants, and taking it to heart sets you on a

> ...it is important to ensure that each ounce of your work can be built into the bigger picture.

course for constant improvement and greater success. So what kind of additional value can you get from your moonlighting work?

EXPANSION PLANS

Here are four simple ways to go from a modest start to immodest success:

1. **Developing templates** helps you to be more efficient and helps you to appear more professional. Greater efficiency leads to your ability to pitch more business and take on more clients at once. Consider templates for any standard activity within your line of expertise.

2. **Ongoing content** should always be in the back of your mind—even with your first small moonlighting gigs. Is there a one-page case study here? A blog entry?

3. **Use client feedback** to improve your services, understand how your work will be used, and to perhaps discover a new opportunity with the client.

4. **Seek out similar opportunities** that can be built via referrals and follow-up work from the client. Also, a small amount of online research will help you discover similar businesses that might be in need of similar services. Note: this is the one time where I suggest that a cold call (or cold email) would be a good use of time

As I mentioned at the start of this chapter, it is far from likely that your prime-the-pump-work and moonlighting efforts will move in a predictable linear fashion. You will make progress, however, if you stick with the plan and communicate openly with those around you. In time, the result will be the start of your independence and enough confidence to really end your formal employment.

PART 3: WHEN TO LEAVE AND HOW TO DO IT

Timing is Everything

Only you can really know when it's time to cut yourself loose and leave your current job. Personally, you have to feel like you have hit your stride with moonlighting gigs and other opportunities, that you're generally healthy and free of new major medical issues, and you are free of major life events like new houses, children, and caring for family members. Continue to think through your decision with those closest to you. Review your Prep Plan and be sure that you are prepared financially and emotionally.

> Only you can really know when it's time to cut yourself loose and leave your current job.

As big as this decision is, the *way* in which you carry it through matters, too. It's too easy to not manage yourself correctly and leave a last-minute impression that could affect your professional relationships down the road. In other words, be a pro. Take the high road when leaving a current job. Burn no bridges. Instead, always be gracious and be thankful to your managers, colleagues, and clients. Remain productive and professional and operate from the right reasons always.

Here are a few more things to keep in mind on your way out:

A GRACEFUL EXIT STRATEGY

Before the curtain comes down on that cubicle of yours, you should:

Make sure you are in best-possible standing with employers and clients. If there are minor issues that can be worked out in a few days or weeks, consider the value of making things right before you leave.

Honor your commitments. Consider hanging on for up to three months if you are you in the middle of a high-profile/high-risk project where you are desperately needed. In some cases, it's projects like these that drive employees away—usually because of the stress. If that's the case, more immediate action might be appropriate.

If an annual review or bonus is around the corner, stick around for what you deserve, but draw a line for yourself. Calculate what it will cost you to stay beyond your self-imposed deadline.

Your Final Prep

In many modern corporate settings, an employee's email account is locked down as soon as employment is discontinued, and in some place he or she is walked directly out of the building by security. Before that happens to you, go through your desk drawers and collect the following—you'll need it.

- names and contact info of current colleagues, partners, and clients
- templates, diagrams, or collateral from which you could learn
- any actual work that showcases your talent, including high-level metrics
- any personal content on your office computer or phone, sending it to your personal account well in advance of your official disengagement

- a memento of some sort that you can look at to remind yourself of why you're doing this when pushing through the most challenging times of the Transition to Independence

Thou Shalt Not ...

Important: I do not advocate theft of intellectual property. My advice is for inspiration only. You will need to create your own materials from scratch and cannot use ideas owned by your employer. Nor do I advocate violating any non-compete agreement you might have with your current employer. Your contact info is useful for down the road only.

Last Words with Your Manager

Before having the "I'm fired!" conversation with your manager, take time to think through what you want because you'll have only one chance to get this right.

THIS IS YOUR EXIT ↗

You may love your work, but remember there are more than fifty ways to leave that love behind. But you should be specific—with yourself and with your employer—regarding what manner of leaving will work best. Especially consider these:

- **Be sure you are 100 percent clear** on contractual responsibilities for both you and employer.
- **Be clear on the amount** of standard pay, bonuses, sick leave, and vacations you are owed.
- **Be sure you know how your benefits work**. Do they terminate immediately when you quit? Thirty days later? Can they be extended by three months? This can be a negotiating point at times and is one of the reasons why you want to maintain a healthy relationship. Extended health care can ease your financial burden during your transition from employee to Independent.
- **Commit to creating a strong transition plan** for your replacement. Create good documentation (which will be helpful to you, too). Sometimes this can be included in a post-employment contract-gig with your employer (see below), and it fosters a positive ongoing relationship after you leave.
- **Is there an opportunity for you** to go from employee to contractor? If yes, consider this opportunity. As a general rule, your bare minimum hourly rate as an Independent should be about one and a half times your current hourly. Again, an arrangement like this can help with your transition by rounding out your freelance work. It also allows you the opportunity to shift your moonlighting into daylight hours.
- **If you are enticed to stay on**, set an outside limit for how long you'll continue as an employee. A whole new lifestyle awaits you once you are free of corporate employment!

SHARE THE SWEET SORROW.

You are leaving not just a job—but a kind of family (dysfunctionality included), so don't be afraid to let a little sentiment show.

After you've settled with your manager—and if you're allowed to do so—physically walk around the office and talk with people one-on-one. Shake hands, hug, or do whatever it is you do. These final one-on-one connections leave an impression and are good opportunities to let a broader set of people know about your next move and how they might help. You might even inspire a few people! Explain your story quickly, exude optimism and confidence, and take the high road.

Leave a note in the inboxes of your colleagues. Again if your employer allows it, also send a final email with a very short good-bye, thank-you, and if-you-need-assistance message. Include clients if possible, include your personal email, and do *not* mention any specifics of your new Independent venture—it's bad form to do so when trying to leave on a high note.

Be somebody to be missed. In all interactions, be a good person. Keep it light, positive, and gracious. Don't gloat and don't settle scores.

Then put your stuff in a cardboard box and walk out of the office building. As the door closes behind, you will be taking your first steps toward freedom and independence. Take a deep breath and exhale. You're about to become a whole new person! I can guarantee it; I've been there.

As the door closes behind, you will be taking your first steps toward freedom and independence.

CHAPTER 6

Step 4: Win and Sustain New Business

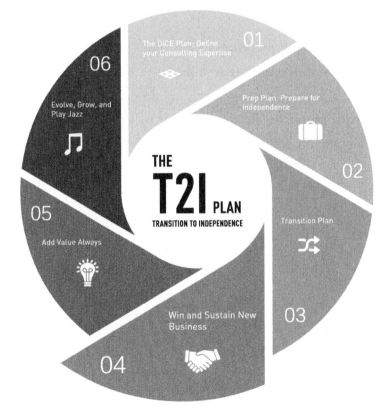

As we have highlighted many times, Independence does not come with a safety net for when work is slow. So, one of your greatest challenges will be to maintain a steady stream of business. The T2I Plan addresses this challenge with a safe-and-slow approach in your transition plan (from the prior chapter). That same approach serves you in the long term, too, by helping you to develop healthy habits that keep you plugged in—via reading and writing expertise-specific content and by being in the mix with appropriate networking opportunities.

While these activities will help to bring opportunities to you, the ability to write an effective proposal is what will help you to close the business and keep your Independence in a state of solid financial health!

I've written many proposals in my time, and on behalf of my clients, I continue to read even more. In this chapter, I'll share with you my general approach to developing and pitching successful proposals. Readers looking to learn more can go to t2iplan.com for additional detail.

PART 1: KNOW YOUR STRATEGIC OBJECTIVES

Living in independence for the past fifteen years has given me the opportunity to really understand the core of what makes my life/work balance sustainable: developing clients

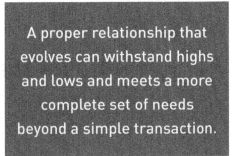

A proper relationship that evolves can withstand highs and lows and meets a more complete set of needs beyond a simple transaction.

who are partners in a relationship. A proper relationship that evolves can withstand highs and lows and meets a more complete set of needs beyond a simple transaction. This might sound like lofty rhetoric, but the results are significant and tangible:

Sustainable (longer-term) clients. You'll be able to continue working with clients whose benefits and interests complement yours.

More repeat business. Rather than having every transaction be a one-off as it's passed along the corporate chain of command-and-responsibility, you will always be in a position to do the final hand-off. Make sure it's pleasant enough to invite a welcome-back handshake.

More referrals. Remember every client is a living, breathing LinkedIn contact with a full trail of other contacts.

Evolving responsibilities (which result in higher fees). Make yourself indispensable. Do more than expected and be willing to become a go-to for whatever your client needs.

Greater enjoyment of your work. Succeeding, remember, is actually fun!

THE KEY COMPONENTS OF A GREAT STRATEGIC RELATIONSHIP.

Experience has helped me to evolve my strategic objectives to where they are today. As you size up any new client or create a new proposal for an existing client, your strategic goals should always be (in descending order of importance):

1. Developing relationships that will extend beyond current efforts
2. Taking on clients that will improve your consultancy (experience, skill set, recognition, referrals)
3. Maintaining a retainer with a client for as long as is mutually beneficial (i.e., as long as you are providing value)
4. Obtaining the highest-possible rate

Read these again. They're important and we'll come back to them in the next chapter. They tell us that you should be selective in the work you're pitching and that you shouldn't always fight for every last dime. Instead, focus on getting good work that will help you to grow professionally. Demonstrate value. Then, in time, you will be able to justify an improved rate.

> you should be selective in the work you're pitching and that you shouldn't always fight for every last dime.

Important note: This certainly does *not* mean you should work for free. In fact, if a client requests free work or at a rate very below market value, politely decline, regardless of the *upside* or *future opportunities*. The alternative is resentment and ultimately a disagreeable parting of ways.

PART 2: GET TO KNOW A POTENTIAL CLIENT

The common first step in any proposal process is an opening conversation with the client.

Your top goal here is to learn everything that you would need to create a meaningful proposal. This includes the client's needs, budget and timeline, culture, primary business model, and general marketplace dynamics.

Your second goal is to sell a little by explaining how your expertise matches the client's needs.

In this early stage, the selling should be just enough for you to be considered a viable candidate. Attempting to close the deal in an initial conversation can often seem pushy and backfire on you, so focus on gathering information and save the hard sell for a later round.

MEETING PREP

You can increase your chances of success by preparing for these meetings. Spending an hour on basic research can go a long way toward making a favorable impression. Here's a seven-part checklist:

1. **Know what you want before you go.** Your meeting will have a much greater chance of success if you have a very simple, specific goal in mind. (Make this something more sophisticated than just "to get some of their money.")

2. **Review the company website** and one or two social channels like Facebook.

3. **Do the same for known competitors** so you're familiar with the general terrain.

4. **Search for current events and news**—the kind of information that would not necessarily be on their more static websites.

5. **Know who you're going to meet.** Look up your interviewer on LinkedIn. In addition to professional details, you might get lucky and learn that you went to the same school, lived in the same town, etc.

6. **Make note of your past experiences** that would be most relevant to what you think are the client's needs.

7. **Draw up a short list of questions.** They should range from the basic to the more probing. Avoid time-eating small talk and the urge to make the meeting into an opportunity to make a friend. Remember why you're there (see step 1). Leaving with a respectful potential client is a more reasonable ambition than leaving with a new BFF and fishing buddy.

Despite your preparation, you should be listening more than talking in these conversations. Let the conversation carry itself and be alert for opportunities to ask questions. Demonstrate knowledge by opening some questions with "In prior experiences, I have noticed that ..." or "I read recently that ...". If you do this successfully, there should be very little need for you to talk directly about yourself in the conversation. Your potential client should come to understand your expertise via the nature of your leading questions.

> Despite your preparation, you should be listening more than talking in these conversations.

Before the conversation is done, be sure you have all you need to develop a complete proposal. This gets easier with practice, but you'll probably need to be more formulaic at first. Don't be afraid to take notes. You will have to determine how many hours per week you'll need, the duration of the contract, actual deliverables, and the specific value-add realized by those deliverables. In addition, you need to walk out of this conversation with at least some sense of how well your expectations on these points would match up with those of the client.

PART 3: FRAME UP YOUR OFFER AND SUBMIT YOUR PROPOSAL

Although this can vary for certain areas of expertise, you should generally strive to submit your Statement of Work (SOW), a.k.a. *the proposal,* within three days of your conversation with the stakeholder. You always want to strike while the iron is hot! If you have followed my advice on developing templates and standard text, this three-day benchmark becomes much easier to meet.

Begin your proposal with a simple sentence (or two) describing the current state and the desired end state (or result) of your client. Opening like this makes clear your understanding of the client's need and helps to get both of you on the same page—always a good thing in a sales process.

A GREAT START.

Although it is just a few sentences, the first section of your proposal will probably take the longest to write. To do it well, you must synthesize what you have learned from your research and discussions with the stakeholders. I often try to describe the need in one of the following categories:

- Give extra support when/where needed.
- Fix something broken.
- Create or build something new.
- Drive excellence, optimization, and efficiency.

Here are a few additional guidelines for you to consider. (I also encourage you to see t2iplan.com for detailed samples and a more in-depth discussion on proposal format and pricing.)

Draw in details from your conversations. This demonstrates to the client that you understand his or her situation and inherently demonstrates your ability to add value.

Keep it short and to the point. The people reading your proposal are busy and are generally unlikely to grind through pages of the single-spaced stuff that you write. Your proposal should almost never exceed three pages of double-spaced text.

Under-promise and over-deliver. Set modest and real expectations within the proposal, especially in regards to how much time you might need.

Set your price at least double the rate you would have received as a full-time employee. One and a half times your prior salary is the bare minimum, but two times your prior salary and higher is common and fair. Remember that as a consultant, the cost of hiring you will almost always be more modest than the cost of recruiting, hiring, and paying taxes and healthcare for a full-time employee.

Eliminate friction in the small things. Send a .pdf version of your proposal because it works on all operating systems. Use a concise and sensible subject line in your email to the prospect. In that email, be polite, concise (again), and thank him or her for this opportunity.

Once you have these basics covered, it's largely in the hands of your client.

PART 4: AFTER SUBMITTING THE PROPOSAL

If everything goes according to plan, the experience of your potential client—let's call her Anne—will go something like this:

Anne had a good conversation with you for thirty to ninety minutes. You came across as knowledgeable and understanding of her situation. You also seemed like you're pleasant and easy to work with. She then had a conversation with another two, three, or five people offering similar services.

Two to three days later, however, Anne receives an email from you. She opens the email from her phone, looks at the attached proposal, and here's what she sees:

- a polite thanks for her time
- a very short statement of work
- an easy-to-understand scope and price point

She's very pleased that the attachment opens without a challenge (no weird versions of Google Docs, no new version of Word...) and she reads it right there. Anne may not realize it immediately, but the document closely mirrors your conversation with her. *There are no real surprises*, and Anne doesn't have to struggle to figure out what you mean or what you're selling. Anne may or may not agree with the price or duration, but she has a good impression that you "get it," and she clearly understands your offer.

If you get this far, congratulations: you've put your best foot forward. Anne experienced no friction and no confusion in her interactions with you. You have successfully advanced the conversation to the next stage.

But let's say it *doesn't* go according to plan. Anne may politely decline. Or, perhaps her manners aren't that great and she simply stops responding to your emails and phone messages. Either way, rejection hurts. Nonetheless, always be polite, accept the outcome with grace, and move on to the next opportunity.

Rejection happens to all of us.

Here is a short list of reasons for rejection that I have either received or doled out (on behalf of clients) over the years.

- *No one* **got the job because …**
  1. The client is more exploratory than you realized. A decision on the whole effort will be considered at a later time.
  2. The client's priorities have shifted—the problem you were going to solve is no longer urgent.
  3. Your contact wasn't the proper stakeholder, and she was unable to sell the whole effort up the chain of command.

- *You* **didn't get the job, because …**
  1. The client already has a good relationship with someone else.
  2. The client went with someone who has more brand recognition—usually this is a safe bet for a stakeholder who doesn't want to create waves.

3. It's simply not a best match in terms of specific value you offer in relation to their needs.

4. Even with all of my great advice, it's possible that you just didn't make a great impression. Hey—you can't please everyone …

If Anne remains interested, however, she may want a follow-up with you to fine-tune or to negotiate price. Fine-tuning is great. You're building a relationship with the client and already adding value by helping her to better understand her needs and desired result. If you stick to your strategic objectives and negotiate with integrity, I'm sure you will get good results.

Stop and take a look at where you are now. This book began with a few thoughts about your desire to improve the quality of your work and the quality of your life. We started at the start, by defining what your consulting services would look like and by prepping those around you for the changes that you were about to bring.

And now you are on the brink of greatness. There are no more foundations and transitions to build. You're out in the wild now, and we're about to take it to the next level. In the following chapter, the T2I Plan continues with best practices for being a better consultant and for putting you on the path to Independence and keeping you there.

CHAPTER 7

Step 5: Adding Value Always

We ended the last chapter by achieving the goal we set up in the first pages of our journey together: becoming a full-blown Independent with a contract

> ...we have not completed our journey together just yet.

in hand. Although this is a significant milestone, we have not completed our journey together just yet. Successful Independents know that there is at least one level higher. There is, in effect, the *project*—which can usually last from one to eighteen months— and the *real project* (or *engagement*)—which can last from three to five years, or more.

TWO KINDS OF WORK

- Projects are often tactical.
- Engagements are usually strategic and therefore support the potential for long-term business.

The engagement concept, you might notice, lines up perfectly with **the key components of a great strategic relationship** we defined in the previous chapter. They're in a box on page 110, but I'll list them here again for your reference:

1. Developing relationships that will extend beyond current efforts
2. Taking on clients that will improve your consultancy (experience, skill set, recognition, referrals)
3. Maintaining a retainer with a client for as long as it is mutually beneficial (i.e., as long as you are providing value)
4. Obtaining the highest-possible rate

Breaking through to the engagement paradigm also supports your lifestyle goals for Independence. It is in this space that you are likely to be considered an advisor instead of a consultant, set ongoing retainer fees, and be most likely to set off-season vacation times, for example.

ADDING VALUE ALWAYS

Beyond completing your project as specified in your Statement of Work, we get to this level by focusing on Adding Value Always (AVA). AVA is my codified approach to the *real project*. It consists of five consulting themes that I (professionally, at least) live by. They are relevant to all consultants, no matter your area of expertise. If you take these items to heart and weave them into all of your work, your long-term success is all but guaranteed.

1. Build Alignment
2. Fight Folklore
3. Enable Success of Others
4. Teach to Fish
5. Understand the Bigger Picture

I'll break each of these down in order in this chapter.

PART 1: BUILD ALIGNMENT

Building alignment is the practice of working with various teams to define the current state of affairs in common terms, come to general consensus regarding a desired outcome, and agree to a specific plan of attack. *Alignment* is the opposite of *silos* and *politics*. Building alignment usually takes a lot of extra effort. The results, however, are more robust relationships between participating parties, which can be a long-term dividend that extends well beyond the project and increases your standing in the eyes of your sponsor.

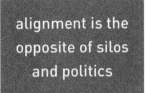

alignment is the opposite of silos and politics

HOW TO DO IT

Building alignment may take extra effort but really it all comes down to three simple things:

1. **Communicate effectively.** Make an extra effort to communicate the same message to all participants and teams.
2. **Speak simply.** Define your vocabulary. You'll be surprised to learn how simple terms like *customer* can mean different things to different people—even in the same company.
3. **Form one version of the truth.** Work to define a reference source for key data points, project status, and other inputs into your project. As an example, I am still surprised to learn that a single department can produce multiple (and conflicting) revenue reports.

PART 2: FIGHT FOLKLORE

Folklore, in my world, is some fact that everyone thinks is true simply because everyone says it is true—a scenario that I encounter more often than I'd care to admit. To explain the damage this can do, I'll share a quick folklore story with you:

A high-stakes project for a large vacation resort (my client) was on the brink of being tanked because we could not get a core technology application (the property management system) to communicate with the check-in gate at the front of the resort. This was a must-have requirement and the urgency was growing by the day, but I couldn't get consistent information or requirements from any of the few dozen people on the project.

So on my next flight to the resort, I simply walked out to the gate and talked with Gus, the old gentleman who had been working the gate for the last fifteen or twenty years. Gus did, indeed, have a computer sitting in the little hut. But when I asked him how he used it to clear people for entry, he laughed. "That thing?" he asked pointing at the dusty old monitor. "I don't bother with that. This works much better." Gus showed me a beat-up old clipboard with a printed report on it. "I ask the girls at the front desk to print out the arrivals for me each morning when I show up. Then I cross people off the list. If someone's not on the list, I call the front desk."

Folklore debunked. Problem solved. The gate check-in system was a legend—folklore—and my project therefore had no such requirement. What a waste of time and anxiety ...

You can fight folklore by asking polite questions and digging around in the weeds a bit. If you can do so without undermining peoples' reputations or behaving like you're one of the hosts of *Mythbusters*, you'll have added value for your client.

PART 3: ENABLE SUCCESS FOR OTHERS

The best Independents work selflessly to enable everyone around them by being generous with pitching in, sharing expertise, and by being sure that the client gets the credit. The effects of this are wonderful and usually long-lasting. Your client

The best Independents work selflessly to enable everyone around them...

improves as a result, the individuals in your client organization *know* that you are helping them to improve, and the other teams (consultants, partners, vendors, etc.) are also more likely to operate at a higher level because of your good example.

The art of enabling this kind of value is in the small stuff. Look for things that you know you can do better or faster than someone else (perhaps you are more efficient with spreadsheets, for example). When you make the offer to help or teach, put it in terms of, "Would it be helpful to you if …? I could take care of it quickly for you, if you like."

PART 4: TEACH TO FISH

Teaching to fish is the phrase found in the axiom about how giving a man a fish feeds him for a day—but *teaching* a man to fish feeds him for a lifetime. It's a great saying, and it's also one of the most powerful ways you can help your client. Here's how to go about teaching your client to fish:

- All of your work should be well documented and reusable by others later, if necessary.
- Teach whomever is willing to learn more about your skills and specialties.
- And do the same with *how* you do things, not just *what* you do. This specifically means to work with others to develop your same level of professionalism and clarity. In particular, you want others to seek alignment and to fight folklore.

If you are particularly successful in teaching to fish, you may find that you've effectively replaced yourself. While it might seem counterintuitive, this usually makes you *more* valuable to the client and pushes you up the food chain to the next most complex or challenging issue.

...replacing your current responsibilities is a good thing for both you and the client!

So believe it or not, replacing your current responsibilities is a good thing for both you and the client!

PART 5: UNDERSTAND THE BIGGER PICTURE

When you understand your project in terms of the bigger picture, you become better at aligning your specific project with your client's broader strategies. This provides value to your client at a whole higher level and may also improve your longer-term prospects with the client. My general approach is simple:

Attempt to understand the true scope of the work. This will reveal whether or not the current work has possible later stages. You may be able to participate in them, but even if you're not, you'll still understand the road map better.

See your piece of the puzzle. In moments of casual downtime, ask client-side colleagues how your effort fits into a larger initiative.

Maintain ongoing homework regarding your client and industry. Continue to read for news regarding changes in leadership, product launches, new competitors, etc.

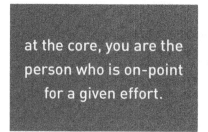

at the core, you are the person who is on-point for a given effort.

Despite the long-term benefits (for you and your client) of AVA, remember that, at the core, you are the person who is on-point for a given effort. You are the one who is not too busy to let things slip through the cracks. Your primary value to the client is simply being "on it" and ensuring follow-through. If you hold to this simple truth and build your AVAs around it, you will always be on the right path.

CHAPTER 8

Step 6: Evolve and Grow

"Work flows to competence." This is a favored saying of one of my mentors. When he says it, he means that doing a good job will open opportunities for you. I have lived my career in

> This guide is built upon a foundation of operating with honesty, quality, integrity.

this manner and can vouch for the results. That's why this guide is built upon a foundation of operating with honesty, quality, integrity. The approach I have described in this book is a selfless one, with the primary focus on enabling your *clients* to be their best and for *them* to get credit for *your* hard work.

But now it is time to discuss what to do with all of the great results and goodwill you have generated by doing your job so well. More specifically, we need to talk about how to keep the good times rolling!

> So let's take everything we've learned and experienced to date and make it work for you.

So let's take everything we've learned and experienced to date and make it work for *you*. For me, *good times* means that subsequent proposals and meetings with potential clients go more smoothly. It means that you are more confident and have steady, dependable business. It means that your experience enables you to put in less effort but get better results. In turn, think about how that would impact the nonwork side of Independence for both you and your family.

Let's have a closer look…

KEEP SCORE

You should be keeping score, quietly, throughout your engagement and/or project. Keep an eye out for victories, big and small. And remember: there's the project, and then there's the *real* project. Your wins therefore may be broader than one might expect, including:

- timeliness of your efforts
- budget/cost of your efforts
- quality of the results (focus on specific data points where possible)

And also …

- improved collaboration across teams
- better-enabled employees and in-house teams
- improved ability to manage projects in the future

I keep this simple list on my whiteboard so that I can call upon it when needed.

TIME YOUR EXIT

All engagements eventually run out of steam. It is the natural order of things, and I embrace the end with the same grace and professionalism that I bring to the beginning. Of course, the easiest indicator of good timing is when you see yourself putting in less time and/or you have completed everything set forth in your Statement of Work.

You'll be the first to know. If you are Adding Value Always, you will probably become aware of this dynamic well before your client does. So take advantage of this and time your exit so that

> It is *always* better to initiate this conversation than to be caught off guard when your client initiates it.

you leave on a high note. It is *always* better to initiate this conversation than to be caught off guard when your client initiates it. When you initiate the conversation, you are Adding Value Always until your very last moment. And what do you get in return? A great reference, of course, and the opportunity for repeat business down the road. On the other hand, if you leave too late, you'll wind up with the perception of being a low value-add or—worse—a consulting leech. This, of course, will burn up all of the goodwill that you had worked so hard to develop.

Provide a great final act. When exiting, I always thank my clients for "the opportunity to work with you" (I do this with each invoice I send, too). I let them know that "I have very much enjoyed working with your team," and that "I hope to do so again one day." And you know what? I mean it. I *have* enjoyed living in Independence while using my expertise with them. And when it is official, I repeat the steps that we reviewed in the "When to Leave and How to Do It" section of chapter 5. I get personal email addresses from people, find each other on LinkedIn, and basically take a little time to say good-bye and thank everyone.

PUBLISH AND PROMOTE

My advice: Take explicit steps to ensure that those who might hire you again (or make a solid referral) are aware of your work and your desire to be helped with future opportunities.

Every project has extra value when you use it to find other projects. So even before you leave a client, you should be working behind the scenes to use your latest work to promote yourself. For longer engagements, it is a good idea to review your work one or two times a year so that your latest and greatest is always in circulation for other potential clients to review.

Freshness sells. The primary reason for keeping your promotional content fresh is that it is easiest to write it up (and talk about it) while the work is still in recent memory. Fresh content always plays well on the Internet, too, of course, in the form of ongoing content (see chapter 5).

Everyone loves a good story. For me, the case study is always the cornerstone of all other promo work. By starting there, I assemble the high-level anecdote and the necessary data points. A good case study is usually just two to three pages, but then I work to boil that down to just three to five bullet points—something that even a busy executive could take in. If I have the opportunity, I'll also seek out a testimonial or two to accompany a case study (hint: some busy execs are willing to lend their names to a reasonable testimonial that you write *for* them).

THE BRILLIANCE OF REPURPOSING.

Repurposing is the epitome of efficiency. You do a thing once and use it again and again. For example, the content we've just discussed (see above) can be used in the ongoing content channels we discussed (again, in chapter 5) like ...

- a template email to potential new business
- your blog
- a guest blog or article in a trade website or magazine[1]
- your website (eg: recent-work page or similar)
- your professional profiles on LinkedIn, Google+, Twitter, etc. ...
- a case study pdf document
- a story to be used as a talking point at your next networking event

Before publishing, check with your clients to see if they can be referenced or not. If not, still publish, but anonymize the clients.

---

1. *There are more opportunities of this type than you might first realize—find the top content sources in your industry and just ask.*

In addition to publishing content, make small occasional efforts to promote yourself to your current client stakeholders. For example, I pass along a humble FYI email every now and then that highlights a moment where I've done a great job in adding value. Or I mention something on the phone. I'm not a huge fan of grandstanding, but I do just enough to help my busy clients remember that I continue to do good work for them.

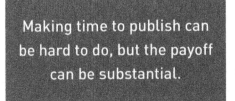

Making time to publish can be hard to do, but the payoff can be substantial. Write while your experiences and familiarity with the data points are still fresh and stick to a template format that will help you to complete the task as efficiently as possible.

BUILD AND REFINE YOUR TEMPLATES

A good set of template documents creates an efficient and repeatable way of approaching problems and managing your work. Templates can be spreadsheets, presentations, or any other format that best suits the purpose. And because they prevent the need to reinvent the wheel with each project, they also free up your thoughts to focus on higher-value stuff, like sharpening your senses for client needs, potential issues, and project scope/duration.

In the end, your templates must be fine-tuned to best support you and your consulting expertise. Always seek to refine (or create new) tools/templates as you need them and be sure that they are …

- functional
- easy to use
- easy for others to understand
- always actionable and results-focused
- broad enough for a variety of different types of projects and engagements

The Classics

Nearly all Independents rely on these templates, regardless of specialty. I encourage you to start with these basics and then create specific-to-you templates as your work evolves.

- **Meeting Toolkit:** As a successful Independent, you must master the basics of running a good meeting. Consider creating basic templates for agendas, meeting notes, and action and issue logs.
- **Project Plan:** A good template plan should set expectations for you and your stakeholders and guide you through daily (or

weekly) activities. It should be *good enough* to set you up as a structured and organized Independent who is ready to add value for your clients on day one but not with so much detail that it needs to be rewritten each and every time.

- **Discovery and Findings:** Have a standard approach for the common discovery phase of a project plus a method for conveying those findings back to the client.

- **General-Purpose Presentations:** Have your logo and client logo in the corner, plus standard slides for title page, page with text, and page without text.

- **Proposal and Statement of Work:** We covered the content of these documents in chapter 6, "Win and Sustain New Business." I'm just suggesting here that you should have a template to make it easier on you for future opportunities.

- **Invoice:** Yes, you'll need a template for that! My clients always like to see my federal tax number on the document. Always send as a pdf (not a .doc or .docx), because those are less likely to be modified in error.

- **Case Studies:** Include sections for *challenge, solution*, and *results*.

Specialized Templates

The templates for an e-commerce expert who works with startups will likely be very different from an agricultural-yield specialist working on a five-year federal government study on new fertilizer techniques. Think about what you need, design the standard approach (plus template), and then make incremental improvements as needed.

If you keep these guiding principles in mind for your templates, they will serve you and your evolving expertise for a long time to come!

MIND THE GAPS

As an engagement comes to an end, many people suffer from a natural tendency to get antsy. It doesn't always feel right to have much less work all of a sudden. You may also feel the pressure to find your next work as soon as possible.

> make the most of your in-between time by focusing on your Independence.

While all of this is reasonable, remember that (1) it takes time to unwind and (2) you should make the most of your in-between time by focusing on your Independence.

Continue to look for your next gig, of course, but do not let that pursuit interfere with your nonwork life. If anything, you should *increase* your time spent on leisure activities. Now's the time! The additional work will come—you've worked hard to help work flow to your talent.

Finally, remember the whole point of Independence is freedom! You've earned it. Don't forget to enjoy it.

CHAPTER 9

Play Jazz

There is one last piece of advice that I can share with you. It's one of my favorites and something that my clients often quote me on: **learn to play jazz.** Jazz is all about playing the wrong note at the right time. The trick, of course, is that you already have to know the right notes—the rules if you will—to make it work. Otherwise, you're just making noise ...

When you're really working and living in Independence, you're in the same mode. It means you have internalized all the best practices—all the right notes—but sometimes you make a decision to do something "wrong" because you have the feeling that you'll get a better result. You avoid dogma (a best practice in all parts of life, I find) and bring a certain flexibility to your methodology, opinions, and techniques. Once you've reached that level, I will have nothing more to teach; I'll just want to play along with you.

I started writing this book when I realized that I had begun to play jazz. It was then that I knew I had something to share with you.

> I started writing this book when I realized that I had begun to play jazz.

I encourage you to take the many points of advice in this book and make them your own. Begin to find your own notes and start to mindfully evolve your professional skills and Independence. When you do that, you're really playing. And when you're really playing, you are tuned in and enjoying yourself.

And isn't that what we all want in work and in life? To enjoy ourselves?

I won't say I'm 100 percent there, but I'm getting as close as someone who works with spreadsheets can get. I have a relatively open and flexible schedule with my young family. We eat dinner at the beach during weekdays. My water-cooler breaks include soccer with the kids in the back yard and short lunches with my wife. Overall, I am happy with the choices I have made. I am happy with my Independence. And, I wouldn't have it any other way.

YOUR JOURNEY BEGINS NOW.

Our first journey together is complete, dear reader, but *your* journey is just beginning! We have designed and worked through the complete T2I Plan, including the following valuable components:

- defining your consulting expertise via your DiCE plan
- preparing yourself via your Prep Plan
- transitioning to professional independence via your transition plan
- writing good proposals
- living as an Independent
- being a good consultant—even a great consultant
- generating ongoing business as an Independent

Independence is waiting for you! I'm living it. I know others who are living it—and you can too.

I wish you all the best and sincerely want to help. Visit t2iplan.com and engage with the T2I community, where you can get additional help and also teach the next generation of Independents. May our paths cross again.

Yours in Independence,
Aaron Zwas

CPSIA information can be obtained at www.ICGtesting.com
Printed in the USA
BVOW06s1430030116

431654BV00001B/1/P